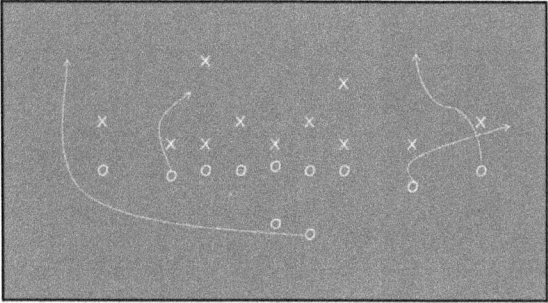

THE SECRET OF SUCCESS

Playing To Win

The Sport of Selling

and

How You Can Win the Game

Allen Guy

SARTORIS
LITERARY
GROUP

A traditional publisher with a non-traditional approach to publishing

Sartoris Literary Group, Inc.
www.sartorisliterary.com

"For when the One Great Scorer comes to mark against your name, he writes—not that you won or lost— but how you played the Game."— Grantland Rice

In honor of two of my greatest heroes, my mother, Thelma Royal Guy and brother, Hardy Vance Guy, I dedicate this book. Thanks for all that you were and all that remains. But thank you most for how you played the game.

Table of Contents

CHAPTER 6

Introduction

After more than twenty-five years selling various products, I've learned many lessons. Among them is the awareness that we as salespeople can never stop learning regardless of whether we're young or old, male or female. Neither should we complicate the sales process in such a manner that overwhelms the audience to the point of confusion and doubt. Perhaps the most important lesson is the absolute requirement to have strong self-motivation to keep focused on the goal—success.

Laid out in this book are simple ideas and illustrations to help men and women sharpen and develop their skills to achieve a more successful career in sales. By painting easy to remember word pictures utilizing sports terminology that both men and women can visualize, this book covers topics you can apply in your day-to-day efforts to build relationships and sell products. Whether your sport is tennis, football, soccer, auto racing or whatever, I believe you'll be entertained as you expand your knowledge and find new motivation to help you land that new account, client, or sale you've been after.

When I graduated from college in 1985, I knew I wanted a career in sales. Even though I had no idea what that meant or even what to expect from a career in sales, I believed I could be a successful salesman; after all, I'm a likeable guy. I make friends easily, and that's all it takes to be a great salesperson. Right?

For my first job out of college, I donned the title Management Trainee. That just meant I was given all the problem projects no one else wanted to tackle. I was assigned jobs that seemed to be headed in a completely different direction from sales. I know you've been there, or maybe you're there right now.

Initially working as a buyer of raw materials for a manufacturing company, I worked hard to implement several new ideas that saved thousands of dollars. I thought I was doing a great job by saving all that money, but my boss didn't see it that way. Turns out he'd been paying inflated prices for goods and receiving kick-backs. Upper management figured all that out, canned him, and promoted me.

Reassigned to create a customer service department, I was surprised to discover the company never had one. As a result, there were no preconceived ideas concerning the formation of this new department. With no direction from management and a little innovation, I instituted and implemented quality standards that instilled in our customers complete confidence in our ability to resolve any issue regarding our products.

After those two successful projects in Purchasing and Customer Service, the company finally gave me my shot at sales. I remember all the emotions I experienced. First, there was the excitement of finally living my dream. Then the doubt came. How well would I do as a salesperson? Would I be successful? Every doubt imaginable ran through my head. Who would buy from me, a young kid just out of college?

Fear can motivate you to do almost anything. But it's not conducive to success in sales, especially if you're afraid of flying, and I was. My first sales call required my first flight. That terrified me. My fear escalated when I learned, I had to meet the president of the company. What was I going to do? That's when I decided experience really did matter, so I asked my boss for advice from all the pointers he'd gained during his years as a top salesman for the company.

I remember Tim, my boss, handing me an air travel card, an OAG book, which lists all flights for all airlines, and a trade publication with virtually all the gas stations and convenience stores in the United States. I was a bit puzzled as Tim's only advice was to call on as many of those prospects as I wanted, just as long as I avoided his customers.

As I began calling on prospects while attempting to sell convenience store fixtures and products to some large petroleum companies, I quickly learned I needed more than just a likeable personality. I also needed discipline, persistence, commitment, and so much more.

After struggling to produce mediocre results, I decided to find an organization offering something different. That's when my friend Lynn introduced me to Kurt, an executive vice president at a bank marketing firm, whose energetic nature was almost as big as his Mount Rushmore-sized ego. But greater than either of those was Kurt's belief in me, along with his ability to encourage others and bring out their best. Although he knew the importance of training and discipline, encouragement topped Kurt's list.

Kurt hired me to sell a "Customer Appreciation Program" to banks. My job was to convince bank presidents to reveal their customer lists to me so I could sell those customers accidental death insurance. Would you surrender your customer list to an insurance salesman? No way! That's exactly what I said. At first I thought the insurance would be impossible to sell. But Kurt got me to believe in myself. He and others taught me how to sell this and other products, and also taught me rules that would help anyone be successful in selling, whether the product was pencils or rocket ships.

In my first year under Kurt's tutelage, I was able to achieve the company's "Rookie of the Year" award. This put me on par with successful leaders and salespeople who had won this award in the years before me. Finally I was on the right track to success in sales. During the next couple of years, Kurt and others taught me even more. And that led to greater success.

The greatest sales successes are sometimes the smallest ones. The greatest rewards are those hard-to-get appointments that finally occur: that best week of sales you have ever had, multiple closes in a single day, and so forth. I quickly learned to celebrate the seemingly less significant successes as much as the "Most Outstanding Calling Officer" award at the president's annual dinner. Many small successes go unnoticed by those around us. Even so, it is important for us to celebrate the smaller victories as much as the larger ones, for the smaller victories are significant victories because they energize you day after day and encourage you to hang in there and succeed.

After two long years of driving 1,200 miles a week, I decided I'd had enough of such a glamorous lifestyle and looked for a more conventional job. I contacted a friend who was human resources director for a large bank in the South. I told him I wanted to get off the road and asked if the bank had any positions available in lending. A few weeks later, I saw my friend, Marty, at church. He asked me to call him the next morning. I did.

Marty told me about a couple of available lending positions and a sales position in cash management. You're probably thinking the same thing I was: "What's cash management?" Then

Marty introduced me to Johnny and Michelle, senior vice president of the department and the vice president directly in charge of the department respectively. They gambled on me, giving me the chance to prove myself. Johnny later said to me, "I knew if you could talk a banker out of his customer list, then you could easily sell cash management."

Almost immediately I relied on Kurt's training in my former job to help me in the new one. I started my new job in 1991 with a stack of manuals that seemed a mile high. I began learning about the bank's balance reporting system. At the time I thought those manuals were the most boring and most ridiculous required reading I had ever done. But what I later realized was that the manuals and the firm foundation Kurt had taught me helped me climb walls of success for the bank.

During the training process I discovered the bank's expectation for customer growth and revenue for the service I was to sell. The prescribed goal was to sell the service to sixty customers in no specific amount of time. I thought, "Where on earth am I going to find sixty intelligent business owners and executives willing to pay for information they can get for free by simply calling their officer?" Long story short, I soon surpassed the goal, taking a product and department once considered a necessary evil to new heights of profit for the bank.

In this book I'll share simple, practical ideas to help enhance your sales ability. Sales is a process. If the process is simplified and executed properly, then the willing salesperson can be successful regardless of personality, background or gender. I'm not a natural born salesperson. In fact, I'm an extreme introvert. Conventional wisdom says an extrovert makes the best salesperson. But I say, "Not so." Having managed and trained numerous young women and men representing a variety of personalities, I've found there are many impressive success stories among them all.

As you read this book, it is my goal to challenge you to grow and reach your goals in selling. Together we'll walk through the sales process step by step. No matter what product or service you sell, you should be able to apply these principles to grow your sales. I've often reminded my salespeople that, no matter the product, whether it's as simple as a paper airplane or as complex as a satellite, the process is the same.

So then, what is the process?

☑ Understand Yourself
☑ Understand the Buyer
☑ Know the Product

- ☑ Position Yourself for Success
- ☑ Plan the Call
- ☑ Implement the Plan
- ☑ Ask for the Business
- ☑ Follow through on the Sale

As we walk through each step in the process, I challenge you to substitute your product or service into the text and to see how these simple techniques and principles can enhance your opportunities. Whether male or female, the principles work for anyone. Demonstrated through sports analogies ranging from women's athletics to gridiron glory, individual domination or team spirit, these principles will equip you with tools to use in a vast array of industries from apparel to automobiles, from software to retirement services and everything in between.

The Quarterback *(The Dominator)*	**The Running Back** *(The Celebrator)*
The Lineman *(The "Whatever" Player)*	**The Wide Receiver** *(The Detailer)*

Chapter 1

Personalities:
Who are you and who is your buyer?

First and foremost, selling involves people, and different people mean different personalities. Understanding those personalities is the first step in having a successful career in sales. Your ability or inability to size up or read your prospects' personalities is vital to you and will set the level of success you obtain.

Many of pro football's greatest running backs have both speed and agility. But the most successful backs are those who can read the defense. Of course, if you're as big and powerful as former Chicago Bears player William "Refrigerator" Perry you could simply run over everyone. But that's not recommended behavior for a salesperson. On the other hand there were the players like the late Walter Payton, or "Sweetness" as he often was called. His ability to elude top-notch defenders was spectacular. If you understand those around you, you too can achieve your own level of sweetness of success when selling.

Remember basketball legend Larry Bird? His uncanny ability to read the court, his opponent and even the ball was incredible. He could anticipate his opponents' next moves and, remarkably, be where the ball would rebound.

Knowing the personality of the prospect hearing your sales presentation can help you anticipate his or her next move, and will help you determine yours. The ability to know how far you can go in one direction or another with a prospect or existing client can give you the upper hand on both the client and the competition you may face.

There are four basic types of personalities most of us have all heard or read about. Since I'm a sports fan and hope you are as well, I look at the four types in a slightly different way.

I label the four types as the Quarterback (the Dominator), the Running Back (the Celebrator), the Wide Receiver (the Detailer), and the Lineman (the "Whatever" Player).

The
Quarterback
(The
Dominator)

The Quarterback

Let us take a look at the first player, the Quarterback or the Dominator. He is the controlling player out on the field. The Quarterback is typically the strongest personality you'll routinely deal with in the sales environment. When the game is on the line, the Quarterback wants the ball. He wants to be in command of the football game and this personality wants to dominate the sales call. He will want to control and direct the game.

Any good defensive player will tell you that you need to watch the quarterback's eyes to know where he'll throw the ball. No, that does not mean you constantly look at the prospect's eyes; but it does mean you should watch his actions and his responses to make sure you're giving him the feeling of retaining control of the meeting.

You may have to remind yourself that there are never two quarterbacks on the field at the same time. If two dominant personalities are in the same room during a sales call, you, the salesperson, will have to modify your approach to see that the two of you don't end up going head-to-head against each another.

The good news about the Quarterback personality is that they're easy to spot. You may initially notice that the Quarterback is first to extend his hand for the introductory handshake. You'll also hear him use words that are direct and to the point, such as, "Have a seat" as opposed to, "Would you like to have a seat?"

You can even size up the Quarterback's personality prior to setting foot in his office. Notice how his secretary or administrative assistant acts. Do they allow others to enter the Quarterback's office without first announcing them? The assistant knows and respects the buyer's level of control and works to maintain that level of control for the Quarterback. Typically, the Quarterback's assistant will let him know before anyone enters his domain. You can think of the assistant as the Center position of the field. Nothing begins until the ball is snapped.

When calling on a Quarterback, he'll want very little chit-chat about you and your company. You may find the Quarterback is very interested in talking about himself or his company so use this to your advantage to build the relationship.

> *"Good afternoon, Mr. Jones. How's your day going?"*

> **"It's going fine. And yours?"**

> *"Likewise, it's been a good day. Mr. Jones, the last time we meet you were about to head out for a fishing trip with some friends. How was the fishing?"*

> **"The trip was fantastic. I caught the biggest blue marlin you've ever seen . . ."**

Great job. You've engaged the buyer in conversation with you. Within a few minutes the Quarterback will want you to start your presentation because the he will want to know where you're going. So many times I have heard this personality simply come out and say, "What do you have for me today?"

It's a fair question, but how do you respond to it?

Human nature says respond to the question with an answer.

"I'd like to tell you about some exciting products we have."

However, if you want to succeed with this customer, you need to retain control of the game while giving your client the feeling he is in control. To regain control, you may respond by saying something like this: "Well, Mr. Jones, I have some things today I believe will increase efficiency within your company and perhaps save your company money. But first I would like to ask you a couple of questions about your company. Is that okay?"

By responding in this manner you regain control of the game and keep the Quarterback in the meeting with his sense of control – (. . . .is that okay?).

At the end of your sales call, you want the Quarterback to believe he's won the game. So when you enter a Quarterback's office, you should quickly familiarize yourself with such items as family pictures, trophies, diplomas, etc. and incorporate them into your conversation. This should accomplish at least three objectives: First, it invites your potential customers to talk about themselves, thus allowing them the sense of control in the conversation. Second, it inspires a more detailed conversation from which you may extract helpful information to help with your sales presentation. And finally, as you leave you leave on a personal note.

> *"Richard, I enjoyed hearing about your fishing trip. Sounds like it was a great time. I hope you get to take that trip again soon."*

> **"We plan to and thanks for stopping by. I'll consider your proposal and get back with you. We'll touch base next week."**

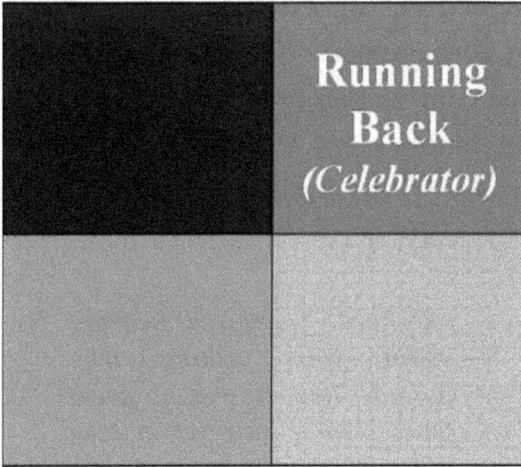

Running
Back
(Celebrator)

The Running Back

The second player or personality type is the Running Back or the Celebrator. Why the name Celebrator? Of all the players on the field, the ones that celebrate success most are the running backs. Each one has his own unique dance or method of celebrating in the end zone like no other player on the field. If the game is tennis, you'll spot the Celebrator even if the point is lost because she'll show the most emotion.

In 1983 pop singer Cindi Lauper released her hit single, "Girls Just Wanna Have Fun." So do

Celebrators. They want to enjoy life to the fullest. Energetic spontaneity engages the Running Back. Life is just one big party and she always wants to be there. Running Backs are fun people to be around because they want everyone to join the celebration and be just as excited as they are.

This personality is always cheerful and usually easy going. My wife is a strong Celebrator so I'm fortunate to be around this positive animation daily. Celebrators tend to avoid tedious details, even though as buyers they know it's their responsibility to see that they're buying products to meet specific needs. You may even find that their attitude is like that of a running back, "Just give me the ball and I'll score!" This course of action is often done without a thought-out plan. They may respond to you entirely by instinct.

Running Backs are easy to spot. If you're meeting a female Celebrator, you may notice colorful, well-coordinated attire accented with trendy accessories. Both male and female Celebrators always seem to be in a good mood. You may wonder, how can anyone be so cheerful? When you walk into their office, you shouldn't expect them to walk over and greet you. You'll likely receive a greeting that includes a warm smile and cheerful hello from across the room.

"Hey! How are you? It's great to see you. Come on in and have a seat. Can I get you a cup of coffee, some water, a soft drink?"

You'll immediately feel welcome when working with a Running Back and you may even have a sense they're your best friend.

"I'm great, Mary. How are you?"

"I'm fantastic. Today has just been so busy but it's been so much fun too. We've had this huge campaign going on all month. The company is just doing so well. Let me show you . . ."

The Celebrator will freely share all the company's good news with you because life is a celebration. You'll find the conversation never lacks for words but you will find it drifting to irrelevant issues and you'll have to gently steer it back on course or you could be with the Celebrator all day.

As you enter the office you'll notice what appears to be disorganized clutter. You may see personal items such as pictures of family members, friends, etc. When working with this personality, accentuate benefits that are of a more personal nature. For example, if you're selling a 401(k) product the conversation may go something like this – *"Mary, the benefit of working with Capstone Financial is that our one-on-one counseling will help your employees achieve their personal financial goals."*

To Running Backs, relationships are extremely important. As you make your presentation, ask yourself, "Am I making a friend with this buyer?"

The difficulty with Running Backs is keeping them focused on the product or service you're selling. Just like the quickness of Walter Payton on the football field, the Celebrators can quickly move around on the sales field. Often times they'll step out-of-bounds but continue playing the game. They'll change the subject in mid-stream and still believe they're right there with you.

"Now with a 401(k), can a person invest in gold? My cousin, Zack said investing in gold is the only way to go. His wife sure invests in a lot

**of gold. You should see the
jewelry this woman has."**

*"Mary, with our products you
can't invest directly in gold
but we offer numerous mutual
funds. Here let me show you.
This fund invests in various
gold mining companies."*

When you see them drifting, which Running
Backs often do, you'll have to bring them back in
bounds gently without any flags being thrown. They
intend no disrespect to you or anyone else; they're
simply being who they are and your ability to
anticipate where they're going on the field will
contribute greatly to your success.

One good note is the Running Back tends to get
excited about almost anything and everything, and
that indicates impulsive buying. So when you're
working with Running Backs, make sure you have
your contracts, agreements, or whatever sales tools
you need to close the deal. Because on the flip side
of things, once you leave their office, they drift to
something else—the next party, adventure, or
celebration. The old saying, "Strike while the iron
is hot" is applicable to the Running Back. Strike
quickly, or lose the sale to the Celebrator's drifting.

A final characteristic you'll notice in a Running Back is they will always have the last word as it's difficult for them to end the conversation.

> *"Thanks, Mary. I'll follow up with you in two weeks as we discussed regarding the proposal. I hope you have a great day."*

> **"Oh, you can count on that. Thanks for coming in today. I enjoyed our conversation. Take care, Mike. I'll see you next time. Bye now. Have a good day…"**

**Wide
Receiver**
(Detailer)

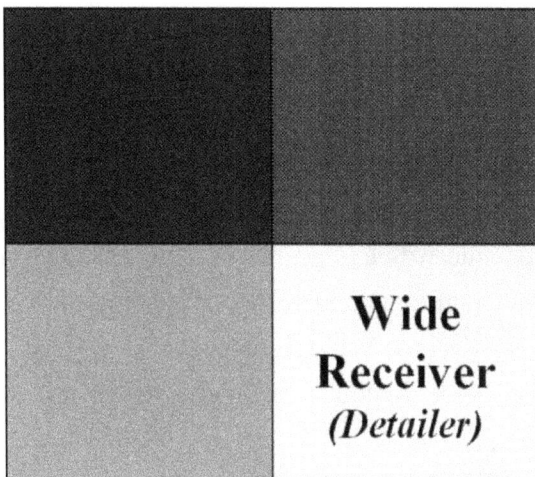

The Wide Receiver

Player three is the Detail Player. I like to refer to these players as the Wide Receivers because they care about their appearance and style of play just as much as they do the plays that are being called. They run their assigned patterns with deft precision, and catch the ball with unbroken concentration.

For wide receivers it's not just about scoring, but about being at the right place at the right time; these are important details for you to understand.

Usually, the wide receiver's position is farthest from the quarterback. This means he must listen intently for the snap count. Wide Receivers, or Detail Players take into consideration your every word.   Their seeming lack of response isn't rudeness; it means they're soaking in all you're saying.

Detail Players want to know every aspect of your product, service, presentation, contracts, etc. In the same way a wide receiver in a football game knows when to go and where he's going prior to the snap, so does the Wide Receiver.

The Wide Receiver isn't one to make a quick decision.

You'll need to load him up with facts that prove to him what you're saying about your product or service is true.   If you're a mutual fund sales representative, the Wide Receiver is the only personality who'll consider reading the prospectus you're showing him.

When you first encounter the Wide Receiver's personality, it may seem cold and distant and about as formal as his or her conservative dress: dark suit, white shirt, bland tie, minimal accessories. Don't be alarmed if the conversation is cool and direct.

"Good morning, Mr. Jones. How are you?"

"I'm doing well, Mrs. Smith. How can I help you today?"

These traits signal a "get down to business, show me the details" attitude. Once you show respect for the buyer's attention to details, then he or she will loosen up a bit. But don't expect them to act like a Celebrator. They'll be cordial, but they are also likely to call you "Mr." or "Ms." and avoid your first name until the relationship is well established. Be ready to get down to business. The value of time seems important to the Wide Receiver, even if it isn't to you.

In football, the wide receiver's role is more complex than any other player's, except the quarterback's. The wide receiver must know the pass pattern, elude defensive backs, and be where the ball is thrown.

Similarly, the Wide Receiver knows how to elude salespeople. Using skepticism, Wide Receivers may cite many reasons for either delaying a decision or rejecting you or your product outright.

Anticipate this behavior and deflect it by knowing details about your product.

> **"Mrs. Smith, what you're saying sounds good. But I'd really like to see data to back up your claims."**

"Mr. Jones, that's a valid point. Let me share with you this study conducted by the Small Urban and Rural Transit Center that shows the impact companies like yours are having on the transportation industry. Can you see from this study how your company can grow in this area as well?"

Wide Receivers may be more sensitive than others; therefore, you must consider every objection as a most important detail to the buyer. Respond to each objection with respect, but follow with a confirmation question to determine if the objection has been overcome.

Wide Receivers are sometimes resistant to change. At the same time, they strive for and expect perfection. They want to know all aspects of the product and read all the fine print. They want to make informed, deeply considered decisions. Despite the intensity of your preparation, the Wide Receiver may indefinitely delay the conclusion to buy. Don't lose patience. Provide the level of detail this person demands and give him or her time to think. Many sales representatives erroneously believe that pauses in conversations mean something is going wrong. But for the Wide Receiver, it's important to allow that moment of silence if you expect to close the deal right away. They're thinking seriously, contemplating the details of the product. You're close to the sale at this point, so be patient and allow the buyer to weigh the benefits.

Picture in your mind a replay of a great touchdown pass. It seems as if everything is silent and motionless except the slow spiraling ball and the wide receiver leaping to make the catch. This is a picture of a detailed buyer making a decision. The question is, "Will the Wide Receiver catch the ball or not?" After several seconds you can ask the buyer what he's thinking. Don't try to answer for them.

> *"Mr. Jones, what are you thinking?"*

Be patient as the buyer answers your question.

> **"I can see how your system will improve our tracking capabilities. But I'm just not sure if your system will be too complicated for our people to use."**

The answer may allow you to lead the buyer to the decision you want. But you cannot become impatient with this personality. Waiting on a Detailer to make a buying decision is like 2012 Women's National Basketball Association MVP Tina Charles waiting for the ball to reach its apex as the referee tosses the opening tip off. If she touches the ball too soon, she creates an unwanted turnover.

If you rush the Wide Receiver, you'll instill doubts and risk losing the sale.

Does that mean you shouldn't try to close the deal during the sales presentation? No. It means you need to entice the buyer to make the decision you want them to make.

Intentional patience coupled with timely, accurate information works like one of Luke Skywalker's Jedi mind tricks. It's simply a matter of being patient and showing the prospective buyer the benefits with facts to prove your claims.

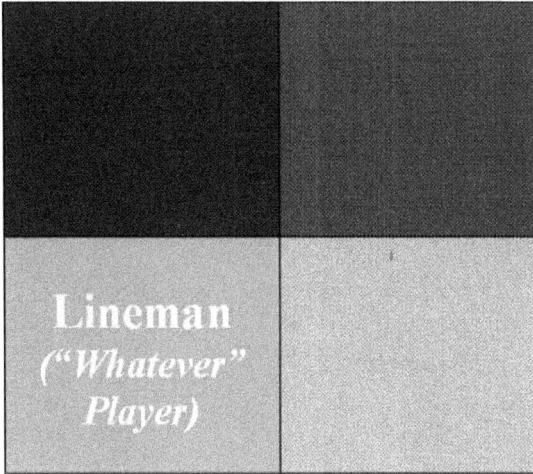

Lineman
("Whatever"
Player)

The Lineman

The fourth type of player is the favorite of former NFL coach and television sports commentator John Madden. I refer to this group as the "Whatever" players, or the Lineman. These guys know their jobs and just simply do it. In a football huddle the linemen are laid back and willing to accept direction from others. In fact, most would prefer someone else lead the conversation and choose the direction. In the same manner a Wide Receiver will delay a decision, so will the Lineman.

In football, linemen don't call the plays in the huddle. They know their blocking assignments and are willing to do what is asked of them. In a sales arena, Linemen are hesitant to decide because they're more comfortable with someone else making the decision. This trait is easily detected by what this buyer says.

> *"Michael, do you see how our service will help your organization?"*
>
> "Yes."
>
> *"Is this something we can move forward with today while I'm here?"*
>
> **"Well you know I'm not sure about all this. I'll need to talk to the rest of the team."**

It is vitally important that you help this buyer become comfortable with what you're selling as well as the decision making process. You don't have to worry much about them becoming comfortable with you because most Linemen are very accepting of others, provided you're not invasive to them.

The linemen in a football game don't receive the notoriety the other players do. John Madden is quick to toot their horns for them, as it is the quarterbacks, running backs and wide receivers that receive more attention than the linemen. Likewise, this personality prefers to remain low key and not draw attention to himself or herself. You won't see Linemen as the life of the party. However, if someone else will get the party rolling, the Linemen are easily influenced to join the party.

You won't see Linemen wearing flashy apparel, as you will a Celebrator. The Linemen will seem to be simpler in each aspect of their life. Don't underestimate this group. Linemen know how things work and are as dependable as the rising sun. When they make a buying recommendation, you can rest assured others take it seriously.

In the sales arena, the Linemen are easy to spot at the beginning of the sales call because they tend to have reserved personalities. They may avoid eye contact, and they won't be aggressive with their handshakes.

When asking probing questions, you'll have to try hard to elicit answers. Linemen prefer to give short answers until they become comfortable talking with you. You'll need to avoid asking closed-ended questions that can be easily answered with a simple "yes" or "no." For example, you may be trying to sell an upgrade to a software system and the conversation may go something like this:

"Charles, how has our software been performing?"

"Fine."

"Does our system provide you the components you need to monitor all inventory and shipping needs?"

"Yes."

"Charles, is there any part of our system you have questions about?"

"No."

In selling software systems you might ask, "If you could change anything about your software or the service you receive, what would you change?" Most Linemen will answer, "Nothing, I don't guess?" You have to drop the bucket deep into the well if you're going to extract any information from a Lineman. But once you do, it's as if you struck a gold mine. They'll tell you things others overlook because the issues seem unimportant to everyone but the Linemen.

"Charles, what exactly do you like most about our system?"

"I like how information is organized. It's easy to quickly find what you need."

"Is there something about our system you'd like to see work better Charles?"

"What would be helpful is if the information could be retrieved faster and allow multiple users to access the system at the same time."

"Charles, that's exactly what I wanted to show you today. Our new release will . . ."

You've now uncovered the information you need to tailor your sales approach and you have a great chance of closing the sale.

Just as if you're on a football field, no matter if you're the quarterback, the running back or the wide receiver, the lineman will block for you. And if you make a sale with a Lineman, he'll clear the path ahead of you so you can score.

In other words, those around the Lineman know the Lineman isn't willing to endorse a product unless there is value in the product. Learning how to influence and encourage a Lineman in a positive way will help you succeed with this type of client.

> *"Charles, Now that you've seen all of our new system capabilities, do you feel comfortable recommending our product to the rest of your team?"*
>
> "Yes, I think this will help us."
>
> *"Great, Charles. I'll follow up with you next Tuesday to see what we need to do to move the project forward."*
>
> "That sounds good, Tom. I'll look for your call on Tuesday."

Notice how the specific probing questions you used to force Charles to open up and talk yielded much information and now at the end of the call, you have Charles more relaxed and freely willing to talk with you more.

Chapter 2

No Two People Are Alike

While there are four distinct and dominant personality types, everyone has traits from all four, with only one being dominant. That means you are unique in the blend of your personality traits, as is everyone else.

In that there are many variations to a basketball team's zone defenses, so there are an infinite number of variations in human personalities. Your task is to determine the unique personality blends belonging to each and every customer or prospect.

Early assessment of these traits will help you efficiently interact with customers and prospects for maximum results, thus increasing your chances of success.

Knowing your prospect or customer, as well as knowing yourself, is important to your success. Coaches and players spend hours viewing and reviewing videotapes of their opponents. Why? Because coaches and players know that for every offense there is a defensive strategy that will work best. Likewise, if you know how an opponent's defensive strategy works, you can adjust your offense for maximum sales.

If you're a football coach who detects a glitch in your opponent's pass defense, then you're going to exploit this weakness and call pass plays frequently. You won't make touchdowns every time, especially if you forgot about the outside linebacker who likes to blitz almost every play.

See how quickly personalities can trick you? Personalities are multi-facetted and always complex. As you learn more about personalities, you'll experience increasing success in sales.

How different personalities interact

Opposites Attract

As you have seen already, the world of personalities is vast. Within that expanse you can quickly find yourself piecing together different jigsaw puzzles from one minute to the next, trying to determine how all these personalities interact with one another.

Certain personalities tend to work more easily with others just as some combinations tend to conflict with one another. When it comes to relationships, we have all heard the old saying: "Opposites attract." Well, it's equally true between salesperson and customer. The table shows the Dominator (the Quarterback) in the upper left quadrant. Diagonally down to the right is the Detail Player (the Wide Receiver). These two personalities tend to compliment each other in the same way a Wide Receiver compliments a Quarterback. The Dominator wants to be in control and make the decisions, but also wants to know each decision is the right one.

For confirmation the decisions are right, the Quarterback (Dominator) tends to trust or rely on a Wide Receiver (Detailer). The Quarterback knows the Wide Receiver has considered all aspects of the product or service and will guide the Quarterback to the right decision. If you're selling to a Quarterback, you want to earn his respect as a Detail Player (Wide Receiver) so the buyer is assured that you'll handle the bothersome details.

The Dominators tend to show appreciation and respect for the Detailers for how they understand the details. It is much easier being the Detailer selling to the Dominator than the other way around. Why is this? If you're a Dominator, you don't want to get bogged down in nitty-gritty details. However, the person sitting across the table or on the phone wants to know all the details of your product or service. You, the Dominator, have to modify your approach to effectively sell this person, the Detailer.

As a Dominator, you don't relish the fine-tooth-comb approach to details. But if you're going to sell the Detailer, who needs this level of explanation before making a decision, then get to know your comb. As a sales rep to Detailers, your patience and attention to details are your best allies.

In the earlier diagram, the upper right quadrant shows the Celebrator, or Running Back. Diagonally down in the lower left quadrant is the "Whatever" player, the Lineman. Unlike the Dominator and the Detailer, the "Whatever" and Celebrator personalities mesh well because neither pressures the other.

The Celebrators tend to work with the Linemen because they're the encouragers and tend to focus more on the positive than the negative. Linemen like to be "pumped up" by those they admire, and want to emulate them. So the acceptance or inclusion of the Lineman by Celebrator puts the Lineman at ease and will more likely lead to increased sales opportunities with the Lineman.

As a Celebrator, you'll find selling to the Lineman easiest. The Lineman sees your excitement about your products and wants to be part of it. In pro football games, a running back will quickly spike the ball in the end zone after running a touchdown and even do a dance. Linemen usually join the end-zone elation and whoop it up with the running back longer than the receivers or quarterback. Similarly, your excitement and enthusiasm about your products and services will help motivate the "Whatever" players, the Linemen, to make decisions.

Likewise, Celebrators thrive near Linemen. As I have described the Linemen as "Whatever" players, Celebrators like anyone who will join their party. The Celebrators enjoy audiences. As a Lineman salesperson, it's vital for you to join the Celebrator's fan club. This is how Linemen score points.

Most Celebrators value benefits of products and services. But if you're competition's products and services are equivalent to yours, then quickly join the Celebrator's team to influence sales. As a sales representative to the Running Back personality, you should celebrate with the Celebrator who buys your product. Help him celebrate the decision and praise him for it. This makes the Celebrator enjoy doing business with you and ensures a long-term relationship that will keep the revenue stream flowing for your organization and the commissions flowing for you.

Clash of the Personalities

Just as some personalities work well together, others do not. They clash. Using the same diagram as before, one can see the Dominant Player, the Quarterback, in the upper left quadrant. Directly across from the Dominant Player is the Celebrator, the Running Back.

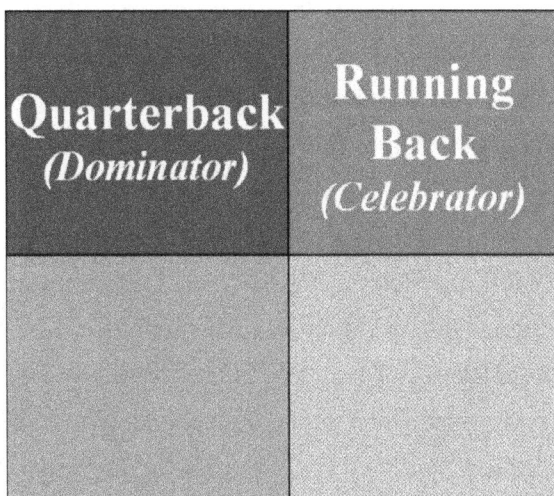

The Quarterback and The Running Back

These two personalities do clash at times because the Dominant Player is focused on the next goal while the Celebrator is still enjoying the last one.

Dominant Players can become frustrated with Celebrators for their lack of focus while celebrating. When a running back returns to the huddle after a long run, he is energized and excited. On the other hand, the quarterback realizes that seconds are dwindling from the play clock, and he wants to start the next play before being penalized.

In each series of downs in a football game, the quarterback must know all the plays and direct the team to execute them flawlessly to help ensure a victory. Quarterback personalities like the role of director. They enjoy calling the plays and seeing them performed as he instructed. But Running Backs are thinking: "Just give me the ball and I'll make it happen." They prefer less direction.

If you're a Running Back and you're trying to sell your product or service to a Quarterback, the Dominant Player, then you'll need to do a little more planning ahead of time. Perhaps writing down an agenda, which goes against your nature, will help you focus while selling to the Dominant Player. The bottom line is you want your customer to sense complete control in the buying process. If you're a Celebrator who drifts randomly through product features and benefits, the Dominant Player will lose that sense of control, and you may lose the sale.

If the opposite is true and you're the Quarterback calling on the Running Back, you'll need to relinquish the reins of control, or at least lead the Celebrator to believe that you have done so.

This can be a two-edged sword.

When calling on a Celebrator, you need to control the call or you'll never move forward on anything. On the other hand, if you're too harsh in bringing the Celebrator back into focus, you may lose the deal.

Because moving on to the next opportunity is important to you, you often won't celebrate victories the way a Running Back celebrates.

You'll therefore need to adjust your style to celebrate with the Celebrator for as long as necessary to make the sale.

Quarterback *(Dominator)*	
Lineman *("Whatever")*	

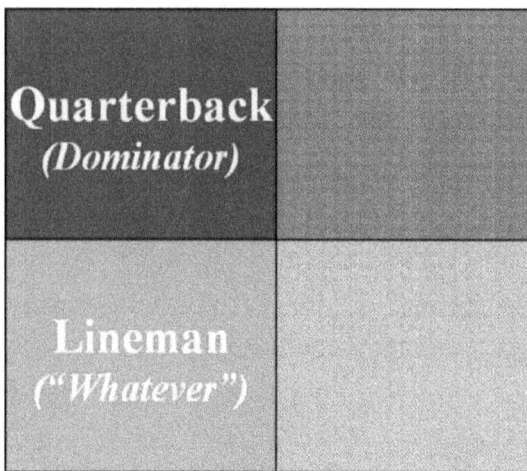

The Quarterback and the Lineman

In our diagram, the Dominant Player, the
Quarterback, is directly above the "Whatever"
Player, the Lineman. These two personalities will
clash because one is full of ambition while the other
is not. Usually "Whatever" Players stay away from
high pressure jobs such as sales and prefer much
more routine assignments. So Dominant Players are
more likely to call on "Whatever" Players than the
reverse.

As a Dominant Player, you must exercise great
patience when selling to a "Whatever" Player. First
of all, they're usually very slow to make any
decision and you seek an answer right away. Many

Lineman are uncomfortable with the decision-making process and even the decision-making authority they may have. As a Quarterback, you'll want to move things forward once the play is called, or once the major benefits have been covered. The Lineman may still be thinking about the snap count and isn't ready to take the next step, so don't rush things with a Lineman.

The second reason the Dominant Player (Quarterback) should be patient with the "Whatever" Player is so his comfort level for conversation increases in the sales process. Linemen usually aren't talkative until they have become comfortable with the salesperson. When you ask a probing question, you'll most likely get an evasive answer until the Lineman reaches his comfort level. For example, if you're calling on a Lineman to sell him office supplies, you may ask, "Carl, what types of stationery does your company use?" The response may simply be, "Letterhead and envelopes." That answer doesn't help much when you're trying to sell cotton bond with a gold leaf emblem.

So as a Dominant Player, how do you get Linemen to talk more? Two words: patient leadership. Remember, Linemen like to be lead, but not too quickly. Try rephrasing your questions with more specificity to elicit a similar answer. For example, you may need to ask; "Carl, I'm sure your company uses 8.5 x 11 letterhead, and standard number 10 envelopes with your logo on them. But what other stationery products does your company use or need?" Now you've given the buyer some ideas to help him answer your question in a way that will make him feel comfortable and get you the information you need to sell additional products.

If you're a Lineman and find yourself calling on a Quarterback, you'll have to move out of your comfort zone far more than the other personality types. As a Lineman, you're likely to be more re-served than others and prefer dealing with people you already know. If you're calling on Quarter-backs, they'll expect you to get down to business right away. Quickly and confidently, you'll need to impress the Quarterback with the benefits of your product. This means lose the timidity or lose the sale. Displaying humble confidence as a leadership trait in the presence of a Quarterback is tricky, be-cause you still want the buyer to sense control in the process.

As a Lineman, your goals won't be as defined as a Quarterback's. So you'll need to better define and know your goals prior to making the sales call so you can quickly convey those goals and objectives to the buyer and keep those goals and objectives in front of the both of you. When a Quarterback has a meeting with a vendor or sales rep who isn't prepared to communicate goals, then the Quarterback loses interest. Understanding that Quarterbacks want to know where the car is going and that Linemen often are along just for the ride will help you make sales to both personality types.

	Running Back *(Celebrator)*
	Wide Receiver *(Detailer)*

The Running Back and
The Wide Receiver

In the battle between the lack of detail and too much detail, which one prevails? These two players can drive each other crazy. The Running Back pays little attention to the details during a sales call. If you're the Wide Receiver trying to sell your product to this type of person, you may need to restrain yourself. You'll need to remain on track and keep the focus of your client or prospect. How? By minimizing the words you use. That's hard for a Detailer, whose attention to detail fosters the desire to share the information. So you should relate only the most notable product features and benefits until asked for more.

For example, if you're selling real estate and you, the Wide Receiver, are showing a house to a Running Back, the Celebrator, you don't need to go into the details of the builder's background. You should assure the buyer the builder has experience but don't try to tell them about every association to which the builder belongs. These things interest you, but they'll bore the buyer and risk your sale.

Another task when selling to a Celebrator is to gently keep them on track. They tend to deviate from the conversation's main point, as they never lack for conversational topics. The Celebrator may avoid the boring details of the retirement plan you're trying to sell by diverting to little Joey's baseball game.

This is both hindrance and help at the same time. On the one hand it hinders your progress. But if you capitalize on it, you can use it to advance the sale. Since you've learned that Little Joey is important to your client, then say, "Do you think what I've presented will impact Little Joey's future?" This approach is non-offensive and will bring the conversation back on track.

Running Backs are encouragers and also like to be encouraged. Wide Receivers tend to be more critical and must not criticize potential buyers, but discover ways to encourage the Celebrator on both personal and professional levels. The Wide Receiver who does this will succeed when selling to Celebrators.

The main point for Detailers selling to Celebrators is to minimize the detail, keep the conversation on track, and not allow critical tendencies to show. What if the table is turned and you're the Running Back or Celebrator trying to sell to the Wide Receiver, the Detailer? Good luck!

You should be organized when calling on a Detailer. Fumbling through your satchel does not impress a Detailer. The more unorganized you seem, the less likely you'll sell your product or service. Respect the buyer's level of organization and attention to detail, and mimic them.

The Celebrator must be disciplined enough to do two things:

1) Put their celebratory attitude on hold; and,

2) Study, learn and be able to recite the details.

The detailer has little time for joviality and frivolity, which takes away valuable time from what he really wants to hear – the details.

You can influence a Detailer from the beginning of your presentation by interjecting some of the more important, yet seemingly minor details of your product. Treat the buyer's minute concerns with respect and let him see that if it is important to him, it truly is important to you as well. These behaviors should increase the buyer's confidence in you.

If you're a Celebrator selling a mutual fund to a Detailer, you should peruse most of the prospectus with your customer. And yes, he'll likely want to have time alone to read the entire document. So be patient.

Caution: Since most Celebrators tend to drift in the conversation, work hard to stay on track. You should have a written agenda to help you focus. If you're not focused, you can't expect your customer to be focused, and you'll risk losing the sale.

As a Running Back (Celebrator) selling to a Wide Receiver (Detailer), remember to be organized, detail-oriented, focused and patient if you want to better the odds in your favor.

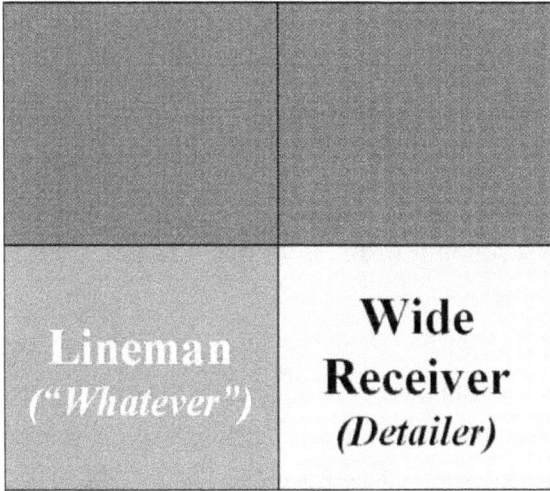

Lineman *("Whatever")*	**Wide Receiver** *(Detailer)*

The Lineman and the Wide Receiver

In the lower two quadrants are the "Whatever" player, the Lineman, and the Detail player, the Wide Receiver. Potentially, these two personalities comprise the most difficult combination in the sales/consumer relationship. The Wide Receiver pays close attention to every aspect of a product or service. On the other hand, the Lineman simply wants to get the job done and isn't likely to show many buying signs.

The details of the process are irrelevant to the Lineman. Even though there are processes and techniques that can aid this person, his focus is to complete the job at his pace and methodology, while often remaining resistant to change. For example, in football, offensive linemen stay in the trenches, concentrating on their individual jobs. They're not worried about the Wide Receivers' routes. Linemen have a job to do – protect the quarterback and/or blow a hole in the defensive line for his running back. Not much changes. Not many details.

If you're the Wide Receiver, a Detailer, selling to a Lineman, then you need a flexible approach. The minor details are important to you but not to your prospect. Therefore, you need to discern when you've going too far with details.

Contributing to potential difficulties between Detailers (Wide Receivers) and "Whatever" players (Linemen) is that Detailers know exactly where they want to go, having considered the entire process, step-by-step. Receivers on a football field know their pass patterns, and try to run them with precision. On the other hand, offensive linemen have a simple job: protect the quarterback. Down after down, even if the offense is unsuccessful, linemen go back to the line of scrimmage and, with the single-minded determination of a battering ram, forge ahead. So when Detailers sell to "Whatever" players, they must be equipped to lead their prospects tactfully around roadblocks and dead ends as they proceed down the road to a successful relationship.

Another difficulty for the Wide Receiver is determining the Lineman's needs, especially since Linemen aren't talkative. Linemen personalities are usually timid and shy at the beginning. They are responders, not initiators. Detailers will have to elicit the information they need to make an intelligent presentation and sale. Then they must be ready for one-word answers to their inquiries.

Suppose a banker who is a Detailer wants to sell more services to a "Whatever" player. He'll have to probe more and lead the buyer with questions that draw responses from the buyer. Let's look a little closer.

> **Banker:** *"What services do you currently have with your bank?"*
>
> **Lineman:** "A checking account and a line of credit."

The banker's question yields a correct answer but it doesn't provide any information to help sway the buyer to his bank. But with much patience and probing, the Detailer can discover his potential customer has multiple checking accounts, investment accounts, a revolving line of credit, two term loans, an equipment lease, lockbox services, trust accounts, direct deposit of employee pay, etc. And the initial response was, *"A checking account and a line of credit."*

> **Banker:** *"Samuel, I'm sure you likely have a revolving line of credit and basic business checking accounts with your current bank, but do you have additional services such as Trust, Investments, safe deposit boxes, zero balance accounts, or other specialty services?"*
>
> **Lineman:** "Yes, we have some trust and investment services with our current bank."
>
> **Banker:** *"Great Samuel. Can you walk me through each of those services you have?"*
>
> **Lineman:** "We have a 401(k) and a sweep we use to pay down our line of credit."

You can see from this dialog the banker has to lead the Lineman through each service to gain the details needed to sell the buyer on his banking services.

Finally, the Lineman's responses grew as the Detailer gained his trust. It's important to note that Linemen like to talk, but fear no one is interested. Show them you care and they will tell you everything and will spill all the detailed beans. You should also let that small part of your Running Back personality surface so you can encourage the Lineman because there is much more information about the person, the company, and the needs of the company to be discovered.

Closing the deal with a Lineman is where patience and trust are vital. In the football huddle, Linemen don't call the plays; they're told what to do, In business, this can be a problem since the "Whatever" player is usually hesitant about decision-making.

Once they make a decision, they will question it repeatedly. They're more comfortable when making joint decisions with someone who is strongly in favor of the decision. Depending on the product or service you're selling, you may be able to influence the sale by assuring your customer he or she is making the right decision.

When selling more expensive products, you may need to involve the Lineman's peers in the decision. If that's the case, you should help the buyer choose the others carefully. You don't want someone with a strong, negative personality to help decide.

When the roles are reversed and you're the Lineman trying to sell to a Wide Receiver, you must prepare for an extensive look at the details. That's because a Detailer wants to know facts about the facts, or descending detail. Not only will he or she want to know what the copier you're selling can do, the customer may want to know how it works a certain way, or even why.

Such details may bother you. But the bother is worth it all the way to the bank. Remember if it's important enough for the buyer to ask, it's important enough to be answered properly. Caution: Be careful how you respond to these detailed questions. Your gestures and voice inflections may send the wrong messages and you could unknowingly insult your customer and shut down the potential buyer. Since many Wide Receivers are skeptical, your difficult task is to build trust. Don't let your rolling eyes or a little chuckle ruin the deal for you.

In the same way a Lineman's personality can hinder a decision, so can a Wide Receiver's.

Detailers are methodical and want guarantees that they're making the right decision based on performance factors of your product and your commitment to stand behind them. Telling a Detailer, *"Oh, we'll take care of you"* sends a bad signal. Detailers want specific information related to the manner of continuing service should any problems arise.

As a Lineman, ballpark assessments are as good for you as specific details. However such speculation won't impress Wide Receivers. They want details. Therefore you should have all conceivable details ready to share. You may need to relay additional information at some point after the initial presentation.

Caution: If you commit to send such information by a certain deadline, meet the deadline. Detailers will not easily forget a missed deadline or a broken promise. The detailer will lose confidence in you. Also, be careful you don't promise more than you or your product can deliver. It is better to promise less and deliver more than promise more and deliver less.

So as a Lineman selling to a Wide Receiver, you should:

- Respect the buyer's "off the wall" detail questions;
- Dig deep into the details of your products; and
- Set realistic expectations.

If you can master these things, you'll be able to turn a potentially negative encounter into a positive encounter and perhaps enjoy repeat business with this client and friend.

Personality Combinations

Once again, recognizing who you are and what personality you're dealing with better positions you to close the deal. Not yet considered however are the almost incalculable variations and combinations of the four basic personality types. Everyone has some level of all the traits. So don't expect to be a master of personality knowledge by having read this book. If you're a fan of Poker you have heard it said of the game: "It takes a minute to learn but a lifetime to master." Personalities are the same. Begin this mastery by first learning who you are. There are numerous personality tests available today. Take one or more of these tests to better understand yourself. If you take such tests, be brutally honest. Don't try to influence the outcome by answering questions the way you think a salesperson should. Flawed answers mean flawed results, and thus an unsuccessful approach to sales. Answer questions openly and honestly so you'll receive accurate and beneficial feedback you can use to succeed in your sales career.

You should also study all personality traits. At some point in your sales career, no matter what you sell, you'll encounter each of the dominant personality traits. You'll also encounter numerous combinations of dominant and non-dominant traits. Everyone is unique. Just when you think you have seen it all, a new combination appears for you to discern and navigate. Understanding people and their personalities is the foundation to selling. The more you know about people, the more likely you'll sell them your products.

$$1$$
$$+1$$
$$\overline{}$$
$$2$$

Chapter 3

Are you prepared for the game?

You now know how to determine basic personality traits and how to size up your customers and prospects. So, what's the next step? Pre-season workouts. They'll prepare and equip you to call on your customers and prospects. Those workouts include:

- ☑ Breaking Bad Habits

- ☑ Learn your products inside and out;

- ☑ Study and know your competition;

- ☑ Write transcripts of presentations;

- ☑ Practice, practice, practice.

Bad Habits Die Hard

We have all heard it said, "If it ain't broke, don't fix it." When you were growing up how many times did you hear, "Just leave well enough alone?" For many things in life we can probably get by with these philosophies. Why worry about making any adjustments if things are working fine?

Even if things are working well for a finely tuned athlete, astute and committed athletes find ways to improve their performance. The slightest adjustments to how a pitcher grips a baseball may add more break in his curve ball. An Olympic swimmer might improve their end-of-the-pool turn to gain just a fraction of a second. However minor the adjustment each modification potentially yields desired gains. What about major changes?

In the movie *Days of Thunder*, Tom Cruise plays the role of Cole Trickle, a racecar driver. Cole is accustomed to driving open-wheeled racecars that he'd been racing aggressively since adolescence. However, because he'd developed inefficient driving habits, his style caused extensive, rapid tire wear. And you can't win races parked in the pits getting new tires.

Harry Hogge is Trickle's crew chief, played by Robert Duval. Harry told Cole to drive 50 laps any way he wanted. Then Harry had the tires changed and told Cole to drive 50 more laps as instructed by him. After those 50 laps, Cole ran six seconds faster and the tires from the second 50 laps showed significantly less wear improving his ability to navigate the track with winning results.

So what does all this have to do with selling? Examine your habits and stop the bad ones. It is especially difficult, however, for those who have been selling for a few years with marginal success to step back and objectively look at their bad habits. The harder they are to see, the harder it is to replace the bad habits with good.

A sales manager and a salesman were showing a product to the gracious president of a small business. The call went well, or so the salesman thought. The manager later asked the salesman if he realized how his hands were flailing about during the presentation. She explained to the salesman he exercised no control over the use of his hands, and that several times during the presentation she felt as if she should duck to avoid being slapped and punched.

The salesman corrected the problem by sitting on his hands during sales calls for three months. He even practiced his sales presentation at night while sitting in front of his hotel room mirror. Not only did he get rid of a bad habit, he learned more appropriate gestures to aide his presentation, making it more effective.

The manager also cautioned the salesman about his body language that was a bit too comfortable in the chair. Such slouching body language tells others you're not interested in their consideration, or worse, you don't believe in what you're selling. Sitting upright in the chair and also leaning forward slightly communicates interest. The salesman stopped the bad habits and adopted new ones. But he never would have known about them had the manager not told him.

For some things in life, "If they ain't broke, don't fix 'em." But as for "If it ain't broke, don't fix it," that idiom itself is broke when it comes to considering bad habits of sales people.

Look at yourself objectively and see what your bad habits are. Ask others to help you discover ways to improve. It may be a little embarrassing, but it's worth a little embarrassment to enhance your clients' perception of you. You may need to restructure your entire sales process to rid yourself of bad habits. You may need to do things that look odd and seem unnatural to you.

Cole Trickle could have continued to drive the way he'd learned as a youngster, but that would mean more frequent pit stops. Even though Cole was a talented driver, there was room for improvement. He learned to drive the car to obtain maximum performance, and he became a winner. And you too can become a winner, or win more frequently if you'll assess your sales habits. Drop the bad ones, adopt new ones.

Learn Your Products

Product knowledge alone will never close a single deal for you. However, the lack of it will quickly lose deals. In 2005 and again in 2009 the North Carolina Tarheels were the national champions of college basketball.

While the Tarheels did a fantastic job on the basketball court, how do you think the same players would do on a lacrosse field? In spite of their great athleticism, and unless they knew the rules of lacrosse, basketball players wouldn't even know how to use those crazy looking sticks.

Suppose you were a receiver in the NFL, recruited out of college with a reputation for having the best hands in the game. You attend spring mini-camp, and all the sports writers are saying that you may be the best wide receiver ever.

You know the playbook better than its author.

You run patterns perfectly.

But does all this knowledge and ability guarantee that you'll score a touchdown or even catch a single pass. No, but the knowledge and abilities surely increase those odds substantially. And without such, you could find yourself running left when the play called for you to go right. You didn't know the play so you were nowhere near the ball to catch it. Similarly, if you don't know your products comprehensively, you'll never be in a position to receive a sale and score.

Carefully studying each aspect of your product or service is extremely important. Your knowledge of your products and services will instill confidence in your prospective buyers.

That confidence factor will make your job easier as you try to surpass your competition.

A complete understanding of your product's dominant features will provide your clients with the most potential benefit. You should also consider the lesser features of your products.

While to you and perhaps your client they may seem small, you never know when or how one of the lesser features will positively distinguish you and your product from the competition and enable you to seal the deal.

The Lesser Product Features

Simply knowing the basics of your product will carry you only so far. In the previous chapter you discovered a multitude of personality traits and variations. The same is true about most products today. Even if you sell something as simple as pencils, today's technology and raw materials can make huge differences in products and services. Each customer's needs are unique, and the tailored look and feel of your product's lesser features may fill those needs.

A top driver in stock car racing may have the edge on other drivers with his nerves of steel and his ability to maneuver a car around the track. His car's motor may even produce more horsepower than the other cars on the track. And if the driver's crew chief completely understands how the smallest tweaks in tire pressure, aerodynamics, springs, etc., can enhance performance, then knowledge of the lesser adjustments may be just enough to push the car across the finish line first.

Racing teams around the world spend millions of dollars investing in wind tunnels trying to find the right combination of adjustments to get maximum aerodynamic efficiency from the car. If you consider Formula One racing, where the track is more complex than a simple oval, teams attempt to find the right set up for every track. Because of the differences in each track, it is important to find the right combination that will produce good straight-line speed but also give the driver control through the tight corners and chicanes.

How do the aerodynamics of your products appear? Do you understand them enough so you can make adjustments to win the race? Do you know when to adjust the brake bias before the next turn? The sales track upon which you race is full of winding twists and hairpin turns. That's why knowing your product's lesser features will help you tweak discussions about them and increase your chances of making the sale.

I cannot tell you the number of sales calls I have made when I expected the call to go the usual direction. But while I was in the midst of the call the customer took the conversation in a completely different direction.

Being able to make a sales call turn on a dime gives me the ability to meet the customers' request and build their confidence level in me.

One angry client was ready to take a large portion of his business elsewhere. But my knowledge of the lesser features convinced the client otherwise and diverted a business loss for me.

Sometimes the lesser things make the biggest differences with customers. I remember my first job after college. I was selling equipment to convenience store and petroleum industries. The company I worked for manufactured fixtures, shelving, display units, etc., for convenience stores and gas stations. Our product prices were more than double the competitions'. Sure, our product was made of metal when others used wood. Metal gave our products a much longer life span. But did the longer life justify paying more than double? At times we had to rely on the simple components of our products to prove that point and distinguish us from the competition.

One of those simple components was our cup dispenser, which was adjustable to fit almost any size cup. This streamlined the process and helped lower prices for our customers to the extent that our cup dispensers became part of their standard specifications for their stores. This automatically gave us an advantage over the competition.

Who would've thought a cup dispenser would make such a difference? Lesser things matter in big ways.

Once I was calling on a prospect that had been banking at a strong competitor for many, many years. The prospect had a tremendous amount of activity in its accounts, which translates into major fee income for a bank. He also kept sizable balances in his account, which meant a funding source for the bank's loans and other investments.

The reception was less than warm. Surely, he was thinking, "Why change now, especially after years of great service?" I was not making much progress with this guy. I asked a simple question, "How many checks do you write each month?"

"I'm not sure," he replied. "Martha, how many checks do we write each month?"

The office manager began searching through their bank statements to find the answer to the question, I asked him, *"How thick is the stack of checks returned by the bank each month?"* He gestured with his index finger and thumb, indicating a stack of checks about two and a half inches high. I responded, *"That's about 400 checks a month."* About that same time the office manager had the official answer:

"Four hundred and eight," she said.

At that moment I saw a different buyer sitting in front of me. His entire attitude changed towards me as if I were someone he needed to listen to. From that point on, he trusted everything I said and the buying signs began to fall into place. By the way, he had a relative in the banking industry who had also tried to move the account without success. I closed the deal and cross-sold several other products simply because I was able to gain his confidence with knowledge as insignificant as approximately how many checks comprised a two-and-a-half-inch stack. Truly there was value in knowing the lesser details.

Believe me when I say to you that you should know your products like you never imagined knowing them. You never know what little feature found in your product will meet the customer's needs and set you apart from the competition.

In a market where almost all banks offer Internet banking services for free, a bank I once worked for continues to successfully sell this service by highlighting a lesser feature of our service, which is often overlooked by sales reps. Its web-based banking system will send an email to subscribing customers or their loan officer with advisories on account balances. This service helps customers avoid additional charges as well as embarrassing overdraft situations. Likewise, the service will alert customers if the balance exceeds a pre-determined amount, enabling the customer to move funds to maximize the interest they can earn.

This lesser feature, which is available at most banks but rarely offered, has helped me sell numerous subscriptions, creating continuous revenue streams for the bank. You never know what lesser feature of your product or service will positively impress a customer to buy.

How well do you understand what one pound of air pressure in the right rear tire will do for you in those high banked corners at Daytona? Is it as simple as a cup dispenser that minimizes quantities? Is it a stack of checks measured in inches that builds confidence? Is it an automatic email that provides peace of mind? Strive to obtain the highest level of performance from your sales car by knowing how and when to make appropriate adjustments and show the benefits of any feature that may result in a sale.

The Dominant Product Features

Know the benefits of each feature: We have covered the lesser features of your products, which are the features I like to refer to as tiebreakers. Those are the point after attempts, the field goals, and the safeties that give you a winning edge.

How well do you know the fundamentals or core features of your products? You probably learned the basics in the first week on the job. Maybe it was the company's six-month training program you completed. Or maybe you're still learning about your products. No matter what the case, the complete knowledge and understanding of your products is paramount to your ability to sell those products.

And no matter how seasoned we are, we need to remind ourselves and refocus frequently on those core features and benefits of our products. Even the best of us become rusty from time to time. In today's ever-changing world of technology, some basic product components change on a regular basis. How many times have you seen Ford, Chevrolet, or Honda broadcast an advertisement reintroducing last year's model? Products change. Are you constantly educating yourself on those changes?

Why do college football programs hold spring training? Why do they begin the season with practice? Why not just show up for the first game and win? Wouldn't it be nice if life worked that way? In the same way a football team must remain in top physical shape and know the plays, we too must remain in top sales shape by having a complete understanding of our products.

Market conditions also change and force us to rethink how we deliver our products and services. Don't take it for granted that you have certain aspects of your products perfected. Maybe you do, or maybe you just think you do. Changes happen instantaneously. It's important you follow and understand those changes in product, market, competition, and any other factor that will impact your ability to sell your products or services.

One of my favorite movies of all time is *Hoosiers*. Gene Hackman plays the role of Norman Dale, a basketball coach nearly washed-out but who was given a second chance. Having been out of the sport for 11 years, Dale shows up for his first practice with his new high school team. The movie, based on a true story, is set in a small, rural Indiana town, where basketball isn't a part of life, it is life. If you haven't seen the movie, I highly recommend you rent it and watch it repeatedly. To me there are so many lessons in the movie about selling, some of which I'll talk about throughout this book.

As Coach Dale steps onto the court for his first practice with his new team, he observes the players scrimmaging. George, a member of the community, is loosely coaching the boys. After encouraging George to leave the gymnasium, Dale says to himself, "Okay, let's see what kind of hand I have been dealt." He introduces himself to the boys and explains to the team his plans to reintroduce and emphasize fundamentals and discipline. Dale dismisses two players for insolence then instructs the remaining players to start dribbling.

Many of Coach Dale's players complained that dribbling and rebounding exercises were not fun and they wanted to shoot the ball. Are salespeople not similar sometimes? We often become so impatient with the details of our products and services that we aren't focused on preparing for the next sales call. Yes, we sometimes see small victories and some of us may even have very successful careers with this approach. But would you not rather win the state championship like the kids in the movie than to have only a winning season?

If you're starting or struggling in your sales career, you should make sure you know and understand your products. If you're the average sales rep in your organization then ask yourself, "What can I do to make it to the next level?" Is it more product knowledge that you need? Or, what if you're the top rep in your company and you're accustomed to having a successful career in selling. Surely, there are no salespeople who believe they are doing such a great job that no more tweaking can improve their sales further?

Teams practice at the beginning of the season as we discussed earlier. You also see teams practice throughout the season as well. You should continue to hone all your sales skills, which includes product knowledge. Continue to learn all you can about your products *as well as* those of your competitors' products. The more you know about your products, the more you can use that knowledge to your advantage when selling.

Despite negative criticism, Coach Dale continued to teach his team basketball fundamentals. People around you may question the way you do things. You may even wonder why to emphasize so much product knowledge.

Just like Coach Dale taught the boys discipline, you too will need to teach yourself discipline. At the end of the movie, the Hickory Huskies won the 1953 Indiana State High School Basketball Championship.

When was the last time you practiced or reviewed your products? Ask yourself, "Am I going to the state championship this year. If not, why? Do I need more product knowledge?" If so, then find it.

Our knowledge of the lesser and dominant features is critical to our success in selling. However, knowing the features alone won't make the first sale for you. You must translate each feature into a benefit for the buyer to see the value of the product or service.

I love sports of all kinds. Over the years, I have enjoyed watching and playing many of them. My knowledge of the games is pretty typical for the Monday morning quarterback. But on the other hand, my abilities are far less than the average athlete. The good Lord chose not to bless me with the abilities of a great athlete. And even though I know the games quite well, I'm still unable to execute the plays because of my lack of athletic ability.

The same principle is true as sales representatives. We can know the playbook inside and out, but if we are not able to execute those plays, then our knowledge is useless. Fortunately, sales skills can be learned much more easily than athletic skills. If you have the desire to sell, then you can learn how to convert features into benefits.

Pretend you sell cars for a living and offer a vehicle rated for 35 miles per gallon of gasoline. This is not a mere fact, it's a selling point that must be emphasized by translating the features into benefits.

For example, you might say to the client, "Vic, not only is this car very comfortable, but it also gets 35 miles per gallon. With today's rising gas prices, that fact alone can mean hundreds of dollars for you and you family each year. How does that sound?"

The excellent mileage is a feature of the car. The benefit is the money the car will save, not to mention the time saved in fewer fuel stops.

You might be thinking, "Well, that's gas mileage and a car. My products are much more complex than gas mileage from a car." That may be true. However, the concept is the same. I deal with software and service vendors all the time. Often I hear their sales pitches and see their PowerPoint® presentations with all the latest features of their products and services. But so often they fail to show me the benefits of their products. In many attempts to convince me of the benefits, they fail to provide proof of the benefits.

Suppose you're selling a new chemical product for use in the agricultural industry? Your prospective clients are farm supply companies. Competitively priced, the chemical controls insect propagation and is environmentally safe. Simply reciting these features won't sell the product for you. You must relate the features as benefits. But how? Maybe this will help if you're selling to Jane, the owner of a supply store.

> *"Jane, our product does two things. It controls the pests that destroy cotton crops. The second is this product is safe*

> *and is environmentally*
> *friendly. Jane, this means*
> *higher cotton yields, fewer*
> *healthcare and labor costs,*
> *and improves the quality of*
> *your farmers' land. Jane,*
> *how does this compare to the*
> *products you currently offer?"*

Imagine you're a sales rep for a furniture manufacturer whose product line is unusually expensive. How do you translate your features into benefits? Or, better still, how do you educate the retail stores' salespeople to translate the features into benefits? I know a salesperson at one of the South's oldest and finest furniture stores, which for four generations has sold high-end, quality furniture. She tells her customers about the quality of some of the manufacturers the store carries. One feature she always points out to buyers is their sofas have *"eight-way, hand-tied structures with kiln-dried wood,"* which means more time was spent building the sofa that provides superior comfort for years to come.

Here's how that translates into benefits:

> *"Martha, I understand other*
> *stores offer lower priced sofas.*
> *I have had other customers*

raise the same questions before. But so many of them realized a well-built sofa provides years of comfort and doesn't have to be replaced as often. You may spend more money now, but in the long run you spend less. Doesn't this make more sense, Martha?"

Knowing how to translate product features into benefits is like a wide receiver knowing when to run which pattern *and* being able to catch the ball. Make sure you can catch the pass by knowing your benefits. You don't want to be the athlete on the field who knows the playbook inside and out but lacks the ability to put points on the board. Learn to translate your product features into benefits you can support with indisputable evidence.

You also need to make sure the benefits are real and measurable. DO NOT bluff through your benefits. What do I mean by that? When you tell someone a product feature will produce certain benefits, you better be able to prove it.

For example, if you claim the paint you sell has one-coat results, then the benefit is money saved by purchasing less and lower labor costs. You should be able to show and support the average cost savings per room with both lab test results as well as customer testimonials.

Face it, most of your prospects shop and buy like the rest of the world, looking for the best value for the money. This means the smart ones will have done their research. Therefore, making ill-informed, off-handed comments about your product as compared to your competitors' could earn you a quick exit from your prospect's office, as well as your own.

I was recently training a new sales representative who wanted to bluff his way through the benefits of his products. As part of my training I use role-playing to teach the sales skills. In each of the role-playing situations, he would always tell me the feature he was showing was cheaper than the competition and would save me money.

Every time I would challenge his statements, he was unable to provide factual data to support his claims. His lack of knowledge of both the competition as well as his own benefits failed to convince me he had a better product. On the other hand, I knew our products as well as our competitors' products, and knew as soon as the words came out of his mouth he had no proof to support his claims.

If a buyer is using a competitor's products, he or she already knows what those products are capable of doing. The new trainee tried to bluff his way through the benefits of our products, which would not serve either the customer or him well in the long run.

If you expect to be in the game for the long term, don't bluff. We've all seen athletes who can make spectacularly evasive moves on the defense and create highlight film moments. However, at the professional level, the defense soon adjusts to the offensive player moves. In the world of selling, you can fake it for only so long. Therefore, make no claims you cannot substantiate. Bluffing your way only works from time to time in poker.

What do you really know About the Competition?

Do you know your competition to the best of your ability? I am often shocked by the lack of knowledge possessed by seasoned salespeople about their competition.

Recently I was talking to a long-tenured salesman. He complained that it was almost impossible to compete in his market because of competition. When I asked him why his competitors were succeeding, he said they offered "better deals."

"Better deals?" Wow, that really narrows it down doesn't it? I probed deeper and discovered he had no idea what his competition was offering to his customers. His definition of "better deal" was he was losing the business and it must be because of a "better deal." How on earth can you compete if you have no idea about what or with whom you're competing?

How many times have you watched sporting events and heard commentators mention scouting reports? Even high school teams and little league soccer teams have scouting reports. Shouldn't professional salespeople? Absolutely!

No, we cannot assemble our sales reps to watch films from our competition's last sales presentation so we can exploit their weaknesses. The way to review the films and highlights of the business world is to ask your customers and prospects what your competitors are doing. I have sold in four completely different industries now and in each of those industries I have found many things in common.

One of those commonalities is that people will tell you more than you ever wanted to know if you'll simply ask. Yes, you're going to have some customers and prospects tell you they won't answer specific questions. So, big deal, there are dozens more who will answer your questions. Don't give up when someone refuses to answer your questions about your competition. If you ask enough questions about your competitors, you'll find out everything you need to know to be successful over them.

The industry where I currently work in is one of the easiest to find out everything you need to know about your competition. Customer's are trusting and willing to tell you about the competition who often reveal all their features, pricing and strategies. I made a call with a lender who was trying to persuade a prospective client to move his banking relationship from the prospect's current bank. Before we arrived at the prospect's office, I asked the lender what rate the competitor bank was charging its customer on the line of credit the customer had. The response was, "I don't know. I cannot ask that question."

Why is it wrong to ask that question? Shortly after the call began, I asked the business owner what rate he was being charged by the other bank. Guess what, he told me right away. We then knew what we had to do to win the business.

It's important to know your enemies' strengths and weaknesses. Are you able to predict what their strategies will be? Learn the competitors' tactics as if you're going to battle because when the business is on the line, you're at war. One common thread sewn into military failures is underestimating one's enemies. When I speak of knowing your enemy, I speak of knowing all aspects of your enemy's tactics and strategies.

Can you dissect your competitors' plans when vying for a sale?

Returning from a vacation I had five messages from employees in a bank department responsible for a sizable relationship that made up a large portion of the bank's business. Fearing they had lost their second largest client, they contacted me to help salvage the deal.

For one week we focused on this one client and one key competitor. Armed with the knowledge of what this competitor would typically do, I detailed nine possible scenarios and prepared a competitive strategy based on those scenarios.

I calculated the risk of losing the business with each scenario and presented a solution with which I believed we had the highest probability of winning the business.

When it was all said and done, I held onto the business. Knowing your competition and anticipating what they will likely do can win deals for you time and time again.

Consider the United States military system. We have the Army, Navy, Air Force, Marines and Coast Guard. But in addition to all that, we have the intelligence community fighting hard to provide key information to our military leaders about our enemies. Any nation, group or individual must consider all aspects of its enemies or else suffer bitter defeat. Why would you want defeat when the answer is so simple?

Can you imagine a professional football team with only one defensive strategy, a short yardage defense? You have only one defensive strategy and the competition has multiple offensive strategies. Who do you think is going to win the game? By halftime you have given up more yards than the New England Patriots give up in a decade and you are losing 200 to zero! That would be ridiculous wouldn't it? Why, then, would you dare make a sales call with only one defensive strategy? Yet many seasoned salespeople do just that every day.

By the way, why do we refer to experienced salespeople as "seasoned?" It's because they've been barbequed by the competition repeatedly.

Some salespeople believe that if they know their competitors' pricing, then they know their competitors. Simply not true! If your competitors are selling on price alone, then eventually poor service or a lower priced competitor will undo them. Know all aspects of your competition. You should know how well they put together a presentation, and make yours better. You should know how they build a business case for their products, and build yours stronger. You should know how they prepare for a call, and be more prepared. You should be equipped to answer questions about your products as well as theirs. Know your competition! And yes, know their pricing too!

What does the competition know about you?

How well do your competitors know you? Are they working as hard to know you as you are to know them? You should always assume the answer to that question is yes. In fact, you should assume your competitors are doing a better job learning about you than you're doing learning about them. Therefore, you should always protect yourself as much as possible.

When you know several companies will be giving a presentation to a prospect, you should try to be the last company or salesperson to make a presentation. By being last, you have the opportunity to ask questions about the competition and at the same time prevent the competition from learning about you. You should also follow up with the prospect sooner and more often than the competition. Don't lose an account because you didn't want to seem too pushy. There is a difference between following up with a purpose and being pushy.

What about your competitors' brochures or websites? When was the last time you read one of their brochures or visited their websites? Is there information in these resources that can help you overcome them? There most likely is very valuable information that will help you. At the same time, be careful you don't give away too many secrets through your brochures, proposals, websites, etc. Have you given your competition all the information they need to beat you in the next fight? Make sure you don't do this.

Place yourself in a customer's office. Do you think customers are relying on a brochure to tell them the details of your service or are they relying on you and the trust you build? Most often the answer is they rely on you. That's if you have done the job of building their trust. If they believe in you, then they couldn't care less what's in your brochure. My point is this:

Yes, you should know your competitors' pricing, but protect yours as much as possible. Limit the knowledge your competitors have about your pricing strategies. We all have marketing companies that want to con us out of our pricing so they can sell this information to our competitors. Learn how to stop these mystery shoppers from obtaining your valuable information; train your staff how to spot them.

Do all you can to expand the knowledge about your competition and limit the information they know about you. Know their pricing. Know how they make presentations, and make yours more impressive. Know how they follow up, and follow up better. Know how they service the client, and service the client better. Know how to defend their offensive moves. Know how to break their lines of defense so at the end of the game you have the winning score, which is the commitment from the customer.

What is written in your playbook?

No successful coach or player has ever set foot on the playing field without preparation. Why would you enter the sales arena unprepared? Every coach and every player who wants to be successful first develops a game plan and is prepared to execute it the moment the teams emerge. It doesn't matter if it's a soccer team for four-year-old girls, the coach has a plan, which may simply be to teach the girls how to have fun. You can bet there is an agenda even at such a simple level.

Every high school, college, or professional football team has a playbook in which the team defines its strategy. Each player carefully studies and reviews the playbook so that on game day, the team is ready. Can you imagine a team in the NFL attempting to compete without a game plan?

Think back to when you were a kid with your buddies playing sandlot football. Even then we drew plans on the ground with twigs. Those were perhaps some of the greatest football plays ever, or at a minimum some of the most creative plays ever devised. Remember writing in the sand, "Okay Johnny, you go left like this and zigzag like that. Pam, you go long and cut across in front of those bushes over there. Tommy, you stay in this time and block. On three!"

Those were fun days and the most creative plays were born on sandlots, backyards, and playgrounds. But, if sales reps wait until we are in the backyard of sales to make plans, it's then too late to realize our best imagination is no substitute for being prepared.

Can you imagine what would happen if former San Francisco Forty-Niner quarterback, Joe Montana, had called plays the same way as kids in a backyard?

"Jerry, you go long. Chris you fade right by the Gatorade stand. Linemen, you stay in and block this time."

I doubt there would've been any playoff games, no division titles, and certainly no Super Bowl rings or trophies to remind the Niners of their success. I can hear John Madden saying: "What is Montana doing? It looks like he's drawing plays on the ground. Is this pro football or what!?" The Niners would have been the laughing stock of pro football, but instead they were the dominant team for many years under the leadership of Joe Montana.

When Montana walked onto the field, he was prepared to win. He knew the plays the offensive coordinator had designed and had repeatedly rehearsed them in his mind and on the field. The team knew how to execute the right play when the situation was third and long as well as when it was first and goal on the two-yard line.

Each player knew the playbook inside and out, and each player knew his responsibilities to ensure success. Every receiver knew the patterns he was to run. Every running back knew his role whether it was to receive a hand off, catch a screen pass, or be a lead blocker. Oh yes, even the linemen knew their roles. Each one knew if he was to pull and lead the running back around the end. He knew if he was to cross block to open a hole or drop back for pass protection.

Even the special teams members, the kickers, punt returners, everyone had prepared to win. If each player didn't understand the playbook and know his role then the Niners would never have succeeded. And unless you're prepared to win at sales, your efforts won't be rewarded with success.

Write your presentation before making a call

You need to know long before arriving on your sales call what you're going to say, how you're going to say it, and when you're going to say it. What you say, how you say it, and when you say it can lay the foundation for success. You should have your words carefully chosen prior to making the call.

Knowing ahead of time what you'll say can and will help you close more sales. Sure you can wing it or shoot from the hip and experience some success. But wouldn't you rather have more confidence knowing you were in control of the game, or sales call?

Preparation can give you this confidence and control. That's why you must write your opening statements. By doing so, you'll know ahead of time how you're going to begin the call, and this helps remove the guesswork and the jitters you may have when making calls. Knowing your introduction ahead of time will help you to relax and enjoy the game or sales experience even more.

Once you know the introduction, also write your plans as to how you'll shift from small talk to uncovering the prospects needs? Wasting a prospect's time with too much incidental conversation shortens the amount of time for more important conversation, so plan the transition carefully. There is no referee in a sales call to throw a flag for delay of game while you try and collect your thoughts.

If you stumble through your sales presentation or drift aimlessly from one point to another, your chances of success grow dimmer and dimmer. This is like fumbling the football. Now you're on defense, and that's not a strong position from which to make a sale.

As you transition from introduction to presentation, you first want to ask probing questions that are pertinent to your product. Do you know what those probing questions should be? Have you written those questions? If you're a candle wholesaler, do you know the questions you'll ask potential clients who own retail stores?

Could the questions be something like this?

> *"What color candles do you find your customers like most?"*

> *"In your opinion, what fragrances do you find are the most popular with your customers?"*

> *"Which displays help you sell more candles?"*

While wax candles are a simple product and the questions listed above are simple questions, probing questions like these lay the ground work for whatever product you're selling whether the product is high tech or low tech - such as candles.

Anticipating the questions to ask prospective clients will help you close more sales.

"But my products are far more complicated than a candle. My customers will think I'm a fool for asking questions like these."

You know, you're right. These are simple questions and are not appropriate for complicated products. I have never sold anything as simple as a candle. But I have always used the same approach when selling any product or service, and have been successful in doing so.

When selling fixtures for convenience stores owned by large petroleum corporations, specific and exacting details were crucial as each fixture had to fit and function flawlessly in its designated space. Many times the buyers were engineers (typically Linemen) who used technical words and concepts I didn't know, thus reflecting their attention to detail. But discovering their needs was handled the same way, and that was by asking probing questions to determine how to make the sale.

While the product or service itself might be complicated, that doesn't mean your questions have to be. But at the same time, your questions must uncover the prospect's needs. Remember that such questions instill a prospect's confidence in you and your products.

So when calling on my prospect's engineers, I asked technical and challenging questions to prove I understood their concerns. An example so such a question could be: "Steve, from an engineering standpoint, what are the maximum sustainable winds you expect your canopies to withstand as you design your facilities?"

On the other hand, when calling on marketing executives of the same companies for the same product, I would use different questions to sell the same products. Marketing executives wanted to know more about how my product would increase store sales, not the product's longevity or durability. For example, *"Mike, how do the graphics on your canopies factor into your marketing strategy?"* Or, *"Mike, to enhance the visibility of your graphics, do you prefer a back-lit canopy or up lighting?"*

However, even the simplest of questions can help make the sale. Simply knowing the quantity your prospect needs may be all that's needed to distinguish you from the competition. You may offer price breaks for large quantity purchases. Just remember to tailor your questions to your products and services with a view of discovering and meeting your prospect's needs. You know your products better than anyone else. You know the appropriate questions to ask. Those questions should probe deeply and uncover all the needs the customers have. Asking good probing questions will set you apart from your competition. Answers to these questions will render information to help increase your sales.

What if you're selling customized software to the medical industry? Should you change your approach? No, you should simply change the questions to uncover the needs from your software package. You still should have your game plan and questions written and ready before the call begins. A sample question for you may be, *"How have you envisioned integrating your patient images with physician instructions, dietary needs, billing, etc.?"* A question can be as simple as, *"What would you like to accomplish with an upgrade to your current computer system?"* I have found questions like these tend to yield an abundance of information to assist me close a sale.

The questions will vary from industry to industry. But no matter if you're selling wax candles or the latest technology in the medical industry, questions will help you close the deal. When you know your probing questions ahead of time, and also how you want to direct the conversation, the greater your chances of leading the prospect. So list your probing questions while you're still in the locker room. And when you step onto the field, you'll be ready to play and win.

Adjustments to the Defense

So, you have written down the probing questions you need to ask. Have you gone far enough to close the deal? Of course not.

There is more work to be done. Have you anticipated what defenses you will face? How will the prospective buyer respond to your questions and then how will you respond?

Every sport requires the coach and players to make adjustments depending on the opponents' strategies. The same is true in sales. No matter how well you have prepared your probing questions or your presentation, the person across the table from you will likely throw out different responses from one call to the next. You need to be prepared to answer those responses effectively.

As we discussed earlier, probing questions should prompt more than a "yes" or "no" answer from your prospect. Each response will be unique in the same way different pro football teams can run different defenses during a football game. Therefore, you need to anticipate those responses and be better prepared than your competition.

Consider a basketball game. How many times can the defense change during one single game? You can play man-to-man or zone. It's pretty straightforward. Right? What about all the other defensive strategies a team may throw at you?

Teams don't always stick to a two-three zone. What happens when they switch to a two-one-two zone? Are you prepared for the half-court press? Have you ever encountered a box-and-one defense while on a sales call? Can you even tell when the defense has changed?

Your ability to adapt to your prospects' countless defenses will enable you to score more points and close more deals. Just as the probing questions are different for each product and service, so are the many responses to your prospects' defenses. And just as you made a list of probing questions, you should also make a list of the different scenarios of possible responses for your products and services. When a defensive back covers your primary receiver, you want to have a receiver in the flats to receive the ball. But don't stop there. You need to know where all your receivers are. So when you're making a sales presentation, you have multiple outlets that make sense to the buyer. If not, you'll be sacked behind the line of scrimmage and miss the sales opportunity.

If your customer responds positively to your probing questions, great! You have the next question or response ready to lead the buyer down the path to close the sale. But what happens when the prospect responds negatively? Have you anticipated that, or how many possible negative responses could come from a prospect? Are you prepared to respond to all of them?

How many times have you seen a linebacker blitz a quarterback and sack him? If you have watched any level of football, you have seen it happen time and time again. How many times have we seen a catcher throw a runner out who was trying to steal second base? If you don't prepare for your prospect's negative responses, then you can easily be thrown out trying to make it to the next sales base.

How you respond to negative responses is extremely important. Those negative responses are the first objections you'll have to overcome in order to close the sale. Keep in mind you're still in the probing stage and haven't even begun your presentation. The right response at this moment can help you move to an easy close during your presentation.

What if you're an insurance sales representative meeting a prospective client who fits the profile your company says will buy a term-life policy. You sense the meeting is going well as you engage in a great dialogue about the client's financial background and needs.

All of a sudden the client says: "I bought a whole-life policy years ago and it turned out to be the biggest mistake of my life. Since then I have never considered buying life insurance."

Certainly, these are not the words you want to hear. You know from this response this truly is someone who needs your product. But how do you respond?

Here's how you may respond to your prospect: "Laura, I completely understand. Many folks feel they should give up on insurance completely because of a product someone talked them into years ago. I'm not here to talk you into anything. What was it about the previous product you purchased that disappointed you?"

This response is the same old "feel, felt and found" response with a little different twist. In this response I've attempted to put both salesperson and buyer on the same team as well as ask another probing question to find out the real objection. My point here is to know in advance how you'll respond to negativity from a prospective buyer so you can neutralize the objections almost immediately.

Your response to negative comments must, with sincerity, command your prospect's attention and offer him respect. If your response to the client is half-hearted and insincere, then the client will tune you out and from that point on the time is wasted for both parties.

f you fumble for the right words to say at the crucial moment, then you have confirmed the response of the client and she'll sense you agree with her. You cannot wait until that moment to know how you'll respond.

You need to know your response ahead of time. If she's had a bad experience before and you stumble through your sales talk, then the client will connect the dots to the previous bad experience and not buy.

If you've anticipated the various responses and formulated your answers prior to the call, then your chances for success have greatly increased. Recall a time when you were watching a football game and the situation was third down and long for an offense that was deep into its own territory. You know as a good coach or quarterback the defense is likely to do one of two things: blitz the quarterback or cover the long pass.

While in the huddle you remind the linemen of their blocking assignments and your play requires the full back to stay in to pick up the blitz. You don't ignore the possibility of the blitz, you prepare for it. Why would you enter a sales call when you know the prospect could blitz at anytime and throw various defenses at you?

The negative responses to your products and services will certainly vary with your industry. They will also vary from customer to customer. Only you know what a full court press looks like on your products. But if you don't prepare for the full court press, you may never even inbound the ball. The point is to prepare and practice your responses so you'll be able to break the press, get the ball down the court to an unguarded basket and score. Practice, Practice, Practice

You have compiled a list of questions.

You have thought through all the possible responses in the same manner a Formula One team calculates its fuel strategy, ride height, and tire pressure for a grand prix.

And like the Formula One driver, who rehearses the layout of a road course in his mind and in the simulator, you must rehearse your strategy. Just as any team in any sport practices in preparation for winning, you too must practice, practice, practice if you want to win.

By practicing your sales talk, you refine the talk, find and fix weaknesses in your presentation skills as well as hone your ability to adjust during the big game. Your mom always taught you, "Practice makes perfect."

While none of us will ever achieve perfection here on earth, we can move our sales presentation closer to perfection through practice.

No World Series winning team ever won without making mistakes. Neither did a team make it to the World Series without repeatedly practicing.

Often times as sales representatives, we become comfortable as we go from sales presentation to sales presentation. Yes, we've seen success and we begin to feel that practice is for the young guys on the team. Right? Rookie and veteran sales personnel would do well to note that successful sales veterans practice throughout the season.

So no matter how seasoned we feel we are, each of us still needs to hone our skills and do our strength training.

You should practice before each sales call. As you can probably tell by now, I am a big fan of Formula One racing. In the off-season and between races, most Formula One racing teams are practicing and developing modifications in preparation for the upcoming races.

Because every track offers unique challenges, the cars are reconfigured from race to race. Some tracks require much more down force because of tight corners and chicanes while other tracks demand greater straight-line speed. Your customers and prospects are the same way.

Each time you step into a customer's office, it is as if you're driving your sales car on a different track. If your car isn't set up for the track, then you're less likely to succeed.

You should've looked ahead to prepare yourself for this track, and then practiced for it. Did you find out as much as you could about this customer? Did you go through their potential needs? Did you determine your race strategy?

I recall driving out to a prospect's office as I was training a young sales representative. As we drove, I asked him to practice our approach and strategy for the call with me. It may have seemed a little ridiculous -- two grown men in a car rehearsing for a sales call.

We talked through the possible call scenarios and finalized our approach for the call. We rehearsed the script and laid out our entire presentation for maximum success.

We made the call and closed the deal. As we left the client's office, the young sales rep expressed his amazement.

"I cannot believe it. That call went exactly the way we practiced it in the car."

It was no surprise to me.

We had determined our game plan long before we arrived at the prospect's office. We made sure we practiced our game plan before setting foot on the field and we won the game.

Being prepared will help lead you to success.

On the other hand, I've made sales calls when I was unprepared. I hadn't planned nor rehearsed my presentation. I went into the game without any warm-up exercises and proceeded to turn the ball over time and time again. I've traveled across the country unprepared, only to waste valuable time and money when I could have taken time to prepare myself and practice for the call.

I remember making a call on the Army & Air Force Exchange Service (AAFES). AAFES has very strict rules about its vendor and buyer relationships. I thought a charming personality and winning smile could sell anything. My company also had a strong reputation in the industry, and surely with those three things working for me I would see great success.

I had visions of one of our latest products being proudly displayed at the front every store they operated. Because of me our company's product would have been shipped around the world to be enjoyed by the men and women of our military and their families.

Well, guess what. I was wrong.

Had I prepared proper responses, I could've shortened the buying window and had many more sales. Because of my lack of preparation, the customer became at best a small account for me when it could have been one of my largest.

The potential with this customer was great. But because I skipped practice that week, I failed to make the most of the call.

Be prepared. Practice. Practice. Practice.

"My practices aren't designed for your enjoyment."

Coach Norman Dale
Hoosiers

Chapter 4

Position Yourself for Success

You have learned about personalities and gone through your pre-season workouts. Now it is time to ask yourself, "Where are you going to find the right leads and prospects to sell your products or services?"

A good athlete anticipates the play and positions himself to be ready to make the play. A good sales representative will do the exact same thing: position himself to receive lead after lead. Are you in position to find good leads that result in increased sales?

One of my best friends from college was Tim. He was a great guy and had lots of ambition. Tim played on one of the best college tennis teams in the nation while attending the University of Georgia. Tim played along side tennis super stars Michael Pernfors and Allen Miller. You're probably thinking to yourself, "So what? Tim played collegiate tennis. Many kids have played tennis while in college and then go on to be professional tennis players. Look at what John McEnroe was able to accomplish."

The aspect that made Tim's career at Georgia so different is that Tim didn't start playing tennis until he was a senior in high school, and later earned his way onto one of the nation's top tennis teams – a pretty amazing accomplishment for anyone.

The one fundamental of tennis that helped make Tim a great player in such a short time wasn't a 135-mile-per-hour-serve. Nor was it his ability to volley better than everyone else. But, like all great tennis stars, Tim knew where to be for the next shot before the ball kissed his opponent's racquet. Tim learned to watch the head of his opponent's racquet and to anticipate where his opponent would hit the ball. This ability gave Tim the split second he needed to position himself for returning the ball and score a winner.

Tim would go to the courts with me to give me, an average 3.0 player, a few pointers about my tennis game. I could never master Tim's fundamental technique of reading the opponent's shots the way Tim could.

A few years back while in my mid-30s, I decided to pick up the racquet again. I joined a league and team of players whose skill levels were the same as mine. My first doubles match as a 3.0 player found my partner and me facing two gentlemen in their late 50s, maybe even their early 60s. We thought our youthfulness would help us defeat those two old geezers. Turns out our powerful serves and strong forehand shots proved to be no match for these experienced veterans. They hardly broke a sweat as we labored to remain competitive. What was the difference? I mean, we had youth and stamina on our side. Why did we not win this match? Like Tim, our opponents, through years of experience, had learned the secret of knowing in advance the place you need to be to make the play. They knew the location where the next lead would be found. I did manage to win a couple of games by adjusting my serve and shifting to my trick serve, which took them out of position to return the ball.

Having played tennis for years, I never could make the transition from tennis to racquetball. In my few failed attempts at racquetball, I discovered the secret of the game is positioning yourself to receive the ball. You have to anticipate from which wall the ball will ricochet and beat the ball to that position. I always tried to chase the ball into the wall. Be warned! Those walls don't give at all! Not only did I leave the courts very sore but also very exhausted having spent energy chasing after something I could not catch. Instead, I should have positioned myself where the ball would be. Are you positioned to receive sales leads or are you spending energy needlessly?

If you have ever watched big league football, you have to wonder how those great receivers like Jerry Rice, Lynn Swan, Michael Irvin and others made so many great catches. Their ability to catch the ball was simply amazing. The biggest key to their success on the gridiron was in knowing the location their next lead was going to be, or where the ball would be thrown.

In football, the quarterback calls the play and the receivers know the pattern they need to run in order to catch the ball as it is thrown. The next time you watch a football game, you'll notice the quarterback throws the ball long before the receiver reaches the target. If the receiver didn't know the pre-determined location where the ball would be thrown, the results would be a broken play, nothing gained and a down lost.

Recently, I was watching a college football game. The play was called, and the ball was snapped. The linemen did a great job of protecting the quarterback, who dropped back into the pocket, planted his feet and threw an incredible pass. The ball had a perfect spiral, great velocity and seemed to be the perfect throw. Down field, the receiver had navigated his way through the defenders and was wide open. It looked as if this was going to be one of the biggest plays of the game. The football reached its destination and hit the receiver squarely in the numbers. Unbelievable throw! Unfortunately, the receiver had not correctly positioned himself. Yes, the ball hit the receiver squarely in the numbers -- the numbers on the back of his jersey. The receiver never turned around to see the ball coming. The result was, of course, an incomplete pass and loss of down.

When a receiver listens to the play, breaks down the defense, and catches the perfect pass from the quarterback, and scores the winning touchdown, it's a beautiful thing for the entire team. The fans erupt into endless ovation. That play is talked about for years to come simply because someone made sure he was in the right place at the right time. Are you reading the plays to determine where leads for your products or services will be found? Sometimes you need to turn around and catch the lead because it may otherwise hit you in the back.

You don't have to be the strongest salesperson in your organization to read the play and place yourself in position to find the leads. Larry Bird was a great basketball player. Not the quickest man out on the court, nor the tallest, but Bird picked up so many rebounds and second shot opportunities by simply playing smart ball and anticipating where the ball would be. He knew the angle from which a player shot the ball and anticipated the location the ball would go after hitting the rim or backboard. Once he knew that, he simply rebounded the ball and shot.

No matter what you're selling, leads are all around you. You simply need to anticipate from what angle the leads are going to come and be there. Often times, leads stare us in the face; but before we make the play, we turn our backs to the lead, overlook it or worse, we let the ball hit us squarely in the back. It's too easy sometimes to be like the receiver who never turns around to catch the ball.

Inside Leads

In many companies today, numerous products are made and/or offered through multiple divisions. Often times those divisions are just that, divisions, divided from one another. Each becomes its own island for fear of being outdone by another division within the company. Why does this happen?

At times, executive management creates an internal environment of competition that's counter-productive to the total organization. Competition within a company can be an awesome growth tool if used properly and not carried to extremes. But when we begin to be more competitive with internal divisions than we do with external competitors, the game is lost. One of our best sources of leads is within our own organization as cross-selling opportunities can abound through communication and capitalization.

As individuals, we, too, can be guilty of creating divisions among ourselves. Anyone in sales, or even considering sales, has some degree of competitiveness within himself. Our competitive natures automatically create walls to protect our domains. But these walls can prohibit the growth of our domain and even erode what we've already built. When we don't take the opportunity to communicate with one another, leads are lost and so are our cross-selling opportunities. We fail to position ourselves for some of the most important plays that strengthen customer relations.

In today's business world, the lines of financial service providers have become blurry. It's difficult to distinguish an insurance company from a bank from a brokerage house. Insurance companies now offer full lines of banking products from consumer loans to checking accounts. Insurance companies sell long-term investments that compete with the brokerage houses. Most banks now, large and small, sell products that cross all three lines, banking, investments and insurance. The brokerage houses are not sitting there waiting for the bankers and insurance agents to steal their customers either. Brokerage houses have been crossing the line for many years. Today they are even more aggressive against each other with discounted on-line services. Some have claims of adding a thousand new customers a day.

I have seen banks struggle with the issues of cross-selling non-traditional banking products. Areas within the organization become very protective of "their" customers. Rather than provide more inter-company services to their clients for risk of offending a customer, salespeople allow their clients to walk over to the competition. If you're not willing to cross-sell your clients, someone is, and in the same way the best quarterbacks have to worry about a free safety coming from nowhere to intercept the ball, we as salespeople must be aware our competition is waiting for opportunities to gain a foothold with our clients.

Communication is the biggest key to successfully cross-selling across company lines. All parties must agree on how the call will be handled. Just as the nine players on a baseball field know what each player's role is and whom he is to back up, we need to know our roles as salespeople.

Take time on the front-end to discuss the tough issues. Define for each other the expectations when handling the customer. Respect one another and respect even more the relationship the referring party has with the external client. Make sure all the ground rules are set and then follow them. Also remember every player on the team has a position and the game cannot be won without the cooperation of the team.

If we as divisions, individuals, sister companies, subsidiaries, etc., can bridle our competitive natures that divide us, then we will find we each have numerous leads for each other. And when we join forces, we are able to strengthen the relationships each of us has with our clients. Cross-selling opportunities are captured, our revenues increase while minimizing expenses, and we have happier customers because we shared leads with one another that brought them products that lead to increased efficiencies.

So then, what do we do? When was the last time you attended a meeting with another department or division outside your own *for the purpose of finding leads*? When was the last time you had lunch with a fellow salesperson outside your territory for the purpose of finding leads?

You say you go to meetings all the time. Well, great! But when was the last time you did it with the purpose of finding new leads?

You say, *"That was not on the agenda of the meeting."* Then place it on the agenda or call a meeting yourself and make finding leads the agenda. The point is to let the people who help support your process know you want and need their help to make you, the company, and them more successful.

Be honest with people up front and let them know you want leads from them. Be willing to set your pride aside and ask for their help. I have a friend who sales for the pharmaceutical industry. Almost weekly she has breakfast or lunch with co-workers to discover ways to team up to find better ways to jointly sell their respective products.

I remember my first few days as a Financial Services Sales Representative for a bank. My boss told me I was expected to sell the bank's new balance reporting service to at least 60 customers within the next 12 months. You maybe thinking, *"Well, big deal. That's only five sales per month."*

The big deal is that the service was priced far above the competition. And not only was the product over-priced; it lacked the same service offered by the competition and no sales had been made in 14 months. The competition's service offered many more features and certainly more benefits. While my customers could access their account information via a personal computer and modem and could print a listing of transactions that had posted over night, my competition offered the same service and more.

My competition's customers could place stop payment orders on checks, download a bank reconciliation file, and store information indefinitely, all for less than half of what I was charging. Their system would allow customers to transfer money between accounts -- and not just accounts at their bank but at other banks as well. Imagine how I felt when I discovered that customers could even transfer money to and from my bank.

Where would I ever find 60 customers willing to pay a monthly fee this high to see their checking account balances, especially when they could call their loan officer and quickly get their account information at no cost? I had to get creative if I was going to meet the goals of the bank.

Uninvited, I began attending business development meetings held by the bank for the benefit of lenders. No one had ever invited a representative from my department to these meetings. I would go uninvited to loan review meetings on a regular basis, constantly crashing the party. I would conduct meetings with the bank operations personnel, you know the ones who never have any contact with the customers. They had great leads for me, too. Frequently, I would meet with the customer service personnel to find prospects, which turned out to be one of my greatest resources. Each meeting positioned me to make plays that would score big for both the bank and myself.

Some of my best leads came from bank personnel who dealt with overdrafts. Most bank employees denigrate check bouncers. But I considered them customers for the product I was selling. Who better to use such a service to manage their money and stop bouncing checks? My hunch was right. Finding solutions for these people helped them better manage their funds and made these customer long-term, loyal customers.

I also found many leads from private, one-on-one meetings with those in position to provide countless leads. In my first few months at the bank, I would go to experienced commercial lenders, the "elite" in the banking world and ask them for referrals. Day after day I would hear the same old response, "I don't have any customers who need your services." I quickly realized this was getting me nowhere. I would have to think differently if I was going to get them to see me as an integral part of their customers' relationships with our bank.

That's when I began going to their loan review meetings and as always, uninvited. In those meetings, the details of all the loans each commercial lender was working on was discussed. I collected company names, contacts, loan information, decision makers' names as well as other pertinent information that could potentially help me make a sale. Attending those meetings and using my process for collecting information proved to be a great move. It positioned me to score big in the same way a professional billiard player looks ahead to the second, third and fourth shots. With this information I was able to look ahead for lead after lead. I could now anticipate the location where more leads would be found.

Armed with information about a commercial lender's customers, I would make appointments with the lenders and let them know I was going out to see their customers. I wasn't anticipating their blessing or asking permission to make the call. Nor was I asking them to go with me, but I was laying the groundwork to transform those lenders into referral machines.

I would then set appointments with the leads I had discovered in the loan review meetings. If the call was a successful call, which may or may not have resulted in a sale (not all successful calls result in closed sales), the first stop I made after returning to the bank was to that lender's office. I would deliver the good news to them face-to-face about the successful calls on their customers. They were simply amazed at all the positive results. Never were they aware of unsuccessful calls because I didn't want to slow the lead-generating momentum down by spoiling good news with bad. All of those successful calls and subsequent visits to the lenders yielded more and more leads. It was as if I was the star receiver in the Super Bowl and could not drop a pass. In no time at all, I had earned the trust of those lenders, and then the leads just seem to fall into my lap. In six months time I could no longer handle all the leads by myself.

Sometimes great leads come from right under our noses. All of us like to think we do a great job in cross-selling our customers. But when was the last time you reviewed your existing customer list and gave your customers a call to sell them additional products or services? Your customers order routinely from you. They have been using your company's products for years. But how often do you call them to see if you could increase their usage of your product? Are you calling them often enough?

I have had both my homeowners and automobile insurance with the same agency and company for better than ten years now. Not once have I received a call from the agent or agency to cross-sell me any product. As a consumer, I'm not complaining. As a salesperson, I'm appalled.

In that same time frame, I've purchased additional life insurance, disability insurance, and other products for my family. However, those purchases were not made through the agency I had dealt with for years, which would have had a great chance of closing the deal. The purchases were through new relationships established through the calling efforts of other agents and agencies. I didn't initiate any of the first calls. Aggressive salespeople initiated the calls and landed the deals.

Have you ever watched a football game and seen a top-notch running back running toward the goal line with no one around, then suddenly he changes directions to look for the free safety? No. The free safety must pursue the running back. Why, then, do we expect the customer to always look for us?

Think about today's busy lifestyles. It seems we have no time for anything. And yes, we all have good intentions of calling our broker, our insurance agent, our banker, etc., to review our portfolios. However, as soon as our feet touch the floor in the morning, we are moving non-stop all day long, and the good intentions to call our financial planner just keeps getting pushed into the next week.

What would we as buyers do if we were only prompted by those wishing to sell us something? Would we ignore the sales rep or make an appointment? Many would make the appointment. Because of this, we sales reps shouldn't lose the opportunity to seek a deal from our existing book of business.

My disability insurance agent called me a few months back to ask if I had a long-term care policy. I told him that I had been thinking about it and that his timing was good. I also told him I wanted to receive a quote from my current insurer. I called my current agent and his first response was: "You don't want that stuff. You're too young and it's way too expensive."

Do you think he made the sale? No way.

Recently I received a marketing brochure from a major appliance manufacturer. I had purchased a new washer and dryer two years earlier. The appliance company knew I had no need for a washer or dryer but the sales pitch was for an extended warranty two years after my purchase.

That's a great way to create outstanding customer loyalty and generate new revenue for the company. They were doing a great job of tapping into a customer base they had already built. When was the last time you were innovative and tried a different approach with your existing customer base?

If you sell cars for a living, how often do you review your customer list to generate new leads? Looking over your list of previous customers or prospects, you may recall Mr. Rutherford bought his daughter a new car for college a year ago.

Did you find out when he would need to replace his SUV or his wife's minivan? Today might be the perfect day to call and ask him if he's ready to trade for a new one. That's exactly how my best friend Chuck purchased his last vehicle.

Sam, a car salesman, remembered Chuck stating he would be replacing his wife's car in a year or so. A year later, Sam called Chuck at his office and asked if he was still planning on replacing his wife's car. Chuck told him he had been thinking about it but had not had time shop for a new vehicle. Sam arranged an appointment and made the sale. Chuck's wife was thrilled with her new car and said it was the finest car she had ever owned.

I bet Sam visits the parts department and service department of the dealership often to find leads for new car sales. What areas in your organization are you seeking more opportunities?

The next time you drive through at your favorite fast food restaurant, instead of being annoyed that the server asked if you wanted to "up-size" your meal, let it serve as a reminder that you should be cross-selling your existing customer base. That's exactly what the fast food chains have been doing for years. And why do you think they don't stop that practice? Because it works and they seize the moment they have with their customers to sell them all they can. Every salesperson should do the same. Review your customer base on a routine basis. When your company introduces a new product, show it to all your customers whether they buy from you regularly or their last purchase was five years ago. Cross-selling opportunities are buried throughout your customer base. Find those opportunities.

Outside Leads:

So you're now attending inter-departmental meetings. You routinely meet one-on-one with others in your organization that can provide you with leads. You're overturning stones that were previously overlooked within the company. You're combing through your list of customers and starting to position yourself to receive great leads. Are you tapping into the leads that are waiting for you outside your organization? Where else can you find leads for your products and services? Leads can come from all sorts of places such as your customers, trade publications, civic clubs, friends, conventions, etc. The opportunities can be endless if you really put some thought into it and dig.

When was the last time you asked one of your customers for a lead? Obtaining leads from existing customers is one of the oldest tools in your sales toolbox, but unfortunately it collects the most rust. Look at it this way: How often do you fail to use this tool and then miss great opportunities? If you have done a great job for a client, why not ask if he has any friends or colleagues who can benefit from the same services you provided him.

When asking your existing clients for referrals, you *must* meet or exceed the level of service you gave to your referring customer. The first time one of the referrals says anything at all that's negative, then the faucet will suddenly dry up without any forewarning or notice. If that occurs, then you're at risk of losing the client who made the referral and you should immediately let the customer know you're aware of your mistake and rebuild the trust that was broken.

Have you ever asked any of your clients who their vendors are? Is it not logical to think that, if their vendors perform similar functions and processes, then they too can benefit from your products or services? If you're able to provide valuable products and services to your clients' vendors, and they know their customer referred you to them, then the relationship between vendor and client is strengthened. You have then won a double-header by solidifying your relationship with the existing customer and turning the referral into a new customer.

What about your customers' customers?

"How dare you ask a customer for their customers! Have you lost your mind? Are you trying to run off my customers?"

The answer to these questions is, "No, I'm not trying to lose my customers, I'm trying to find more to serve." You see, if I provide service to my customers' clients in the same way my customers provide service to their clients, then I have created a triple win. First, my customer sees my commitment to provide superior products and services not only to him, but also to every customer with whom I do business. Second, I have once again strengthened the relationship between the other two parties. Finally, I have developed some new relationships.

My second job in sales was working with a bank marketing company, convincing bank presidents to give me the names and addresses of their customers. Because my company and I placed service quality at the top of our agenda, I cannot tell you the number of times I heard from bank executives who had heard great success stories from their customers as to how pleased they were with our company. When such is the case, you can ask your customer for their customers as long as you place the new relationship above all others.

What about publications, marketing programs, and other resources to discover leads outside your company walls? Are you involved in civic, church, professional or any other types of groups that meet on a regular basis? Are you fully utilizing social media? Do you have any friends? Of course you do. Why not ask people within these groups for leads?

No matter to what industry you belong, most likely there is a trade publication to read or association to join. Many such publications offer numerous leads, and so do annual conferences or conventions.

I attended a banking conference in another state. During the convention, I refused to overlook any opportunity to find leads. Many of my competitors had booths in the exhibit hall staffed with numerous bank representatives and product information. While attending one of the open lunches, I asked a gentleman if I could join him. He politely agreed and I sat down to his right for an enjoyable lunch, conference speaker, and prospect.

A few moments later, two other gentlemen sat down to my right. I struck up a conversation with the gentleman to my left as well as with the two gentlemen to my right and quickly discovered the gentleman on my left was a customer of the gentlemen on my right. I love a challenge, and when I realized I had the chance to steal a customer literally from under the noses of my competition, my mouth started watering - and not from the conference chicken.

Before lunch was over, I had a lead to carry back to one of our lenders for a $15,000,000 loan opportunity.

Yes, have fun at conferences and conventions. Let them recharge your batteries. Use them to build your network of friends and associates, but also keep your eyes open for leads and opportunities to sell your products. Leads are all around. You simply have to be pro-active in discovering those leads.

So, you've attended the Sorority Alumni meetings for more than 15 years and you know any day now one of your sisters is going to do some business with you. Besides, the sisters all know you. They know exactly what you do and the fact that you're a part of the Sorority means they'll automatically buy from you. Right?

We all attend these meetings for two reasons: First, we care about our community and want to support it, which should be your top priority when joining a fraternal or civic organization. Second, we want to expand our network and find ways to grow our business. But unfortunately, most of us fail to seize opportunities from within these organizations and allow business to slip between our fingers.

"Well everyone in the Lion's Club knows I work for _____. If they need something, they'll let me know." So what if everyone knows who you are and what you do. That fact still doesn't guarantee you any business from them. You have to work for the business and ask for the leads.

In the same way a pro football receiver must extend his hands and arms to grab the pass from the quarterback, you too have to extend the invitation to others to do business with you or else the ball may hit you squarely in the numbers on the back of your jersey.

This may come in the form of a conversation you overhear that goes something like this: *"I'm so glad we upgraded the computers in our office. Productivity has increased 35 percent."* And you say to yourself, *"But wait. You needed computers? I sell computers. Why did you, my civic club friend, not buy computers from me?"*

It's because you failed to ask your civic club friend to do business with you, and someone outside the club did. You must position yourself to receive leads, and part of that positioning includes asking people to do business with you. Simply sitting in a coffee shop each morning isn't going to generate sales.

Are you getting my point? Place yourself in position to uncover leads and then follow through on those leads.

What about your friends, your Bunco group, your tennis team? Do you ever talk to them about your business? I don't mean simply having a casual conversation about your business; I mean for the purpose of generating leads. Your friends know you better than anyone else and they know your capabilities.

These are the people who truly believe in you and what you can accomplish. Make the most of that at your next dinner party. Be intentional about generating a couple of leads from your friends. Then enjoy the evening and let them know how much you appreciate the friendship.

Another source of leads from the outside is your local newspaper or regional business journal. Are you looking through the newspaper just to catch up on your favorite sports team or to find at what prices your stocks closed?

Are you looking through newspapers to read only the bad news in your community when you could be using it to find more leads?

Each month I receive a business publication from the farming area of my state. I look through the local business journal and discover numerous leads to pass to sales representatives. In this publication I've never seen an article or advertisement from someone saying they wanted to borrow money, subscribe to other financial services, purchase insurance or even buy a tractor (with the exception of public entities that are required to do so by law).

What I have seen are articles about people and businesses in the community or region. These articles often give information about these individuals or business you can convert into leads for your products or services. For example, if you see an article about a business expanding its facility by 50,000 square feet, then there is a good chance they will need to borrow money, increase their insurance coverage, purchase building materials such as concrete, steal, and so on. What products do you sell that could help them?

Recently I was consulting with a small business experiencing growing pains due to an explosive take off of their products. The state's largest newspaper featured an article about the business owner's success. It was shocking to me that in the weeks following the article only one vendor called on this emerging company. It was a freight carrier.

Where were the insurance agents with the product liability policies? Where were the box suppliers ready to sell packaging products? Where were the bankers seeking to capitalize on the opportunity? We all assume the customer has everything in place. The reality is most small businesses need expert advice from those who are knowledgeable. These opportunities can result in huge gains for the sales reps that dare pick up the phone and make an appointment.

Maybe you see an advertisement to hire employees for a third shift. Perhaps it's time for that company to look at a Simple IRA, a 401(k) plan, or other products that could help its employees. Could they use the security services you sell? What about the company's changing health insurance needs? Is it time the company reconsidered those plans? The possibilities are endless if we will only open our eyes and look at the things we do each day in a different light.

As salespeople, we must seek opportunities and not wait for those opportunities to seek us. We cannot wait for customers to call us.

My point is this. There are leads all around you. There are both internal and external leads available to you. Both possess abundant opportunities for you. Are you positioned to receive those leads? We must be in position to receive leads and then extend our hands and arms to catch the pass and score. Are you extending your hands and arms to receive those leads? If not, why?

Chapter 5

What steps will you take to make the sale?

Football games are divided into four quarters. Baseball games usually last nine innings. If you're a racecar driver, you have a certain number of laps to complete or a time frame in which to compete. Likewise, a sales call has its own set of periods or segments. I believe those periods are divided into five distinct, yet intertwined periods. What are the periods and how are they intertwined?

The periods can be broken down like this:

> I. First Quarter - Defining your goals for the call
>
> II. Second Quarter - Building the foundation
>
> III. Third Quarter - Uncovering the needs
>
> IV. Fourth Quarter - Presenting the right solution

V. Overtime - Closing the sale

The periods are intertwined and build upon one another through the sales presentation or process. Most of us have heard the "ABC's of Selling." This refers to **A**lways **B**e **C**losing. It's true. As salespeople, we should always be working toward the close; and to do so, we must first intertwine the building blocks or periods of our call.

Throughout each period of the sales call, you should be defining where you want to go, uncovering the path to get you there, asking questions that move you in the right direction, and presenting a tailored solution for the prospect. Whether to yourself during your planning period or in front of the client throughout each step of the sales process, asking questions is important to help you formulate the right close at the right time.

The questions you ask in each period should provide feedback about your goals, the person with whom you're dealing, their company, and their needs in relation to your products or services. As you gather information from these questions, you may use it right away. Or, you may need to store the information for use later in the conversation to help you with the sale.

The information you gain through periods one, two, and three should help build toward the close, which are periods four and five. It isn't always the last team to score points that wins the game. Sometimes the early periods are so fruitful that the final period is easy. Have you ever seen a team run a score up so fast in the first quarter of a football game that the opposing team never had a chance to regain the lead? Why not run up the score early when selling? By asking questions that build upon one another through each period of the sales game, you're building for the close and make it much easier to sell your product or service.

So let's take a close look at each of the sales periods, or quarters, to see how each period builds upon the other and moves closer to the goal line, or sale. We'll also talk about the types of questions you'll use to gather information to break down the opponent's defenses.

First Quarter:
Defining your goals for the call

The first quarter of a sales call occurs before you ever set foot in the client's office, before the prospect ever enters your store, or before you ever pick up the telephone.

You must define your goals far in advance of any contact with the prospect.

You may be thinking the obvious goal is to sell the client your product or service. That's true, but what if your product or service is such that a one-call sales cycle is impossible. Then if your goal is to sell the customer on the first call, you're in for some real disappointment. By setting other goals along with the ultimate goal of selling the customer, you can experience more and more successes and also build a pipeline to yield far more sales than if your only approach is to sell everyone you meet on the first call.

In a job I had selling specialized financial services for a bank, I made numerous calls on prospects that had banked elsewhere for years. Usually, my prospects were very happy with their existing bank. They had established automatic withdrawals with trading partners, and so to move their business to another bank required much work on their part, or so they thought. Asking the prospect to change banks on the first sales call can be done, but it isn't likely to yield many accounts.

Once when I was training a new sales representative, Mary, she made an appointment with a prospect who had been doing business with another bank since he started his business. He was happy with the service and believed the price was competitive. Also, his wife enjoyed the convenience of the other bank's Internet banking services. With all that in mind, the prospect was willing to meet with us.

Prior to the call, Mary and I sat down to discuss the call. I asked, *"What are your goals for the call?"*

Her one and only goal was to get the customer into the bank to open an account. While I was thrilled with her enthusiasm, I didn't want to see the wind knocked out of her sails. I suggested we define some other goals for the call as well. In professional football, it is the goal of both teams to win on Sunday afternoon. However, the coach and players have other goals as well. The first goal may be to stop the opposition on its opening drive. Mary and I discussed some other goals and before we left for the prospect's office. We had four:

> 1. Determine the services the customer is using at the other bank
>
> 2. Determine if the competition has any weaknesses in the relationship
>
> 3. Obtain copies of the customer's bank statements

4. Get the customer in the branch to
open an account.

Armed with these goals, we proceeded. As we met with the prospect, we quickly learned all the services he was using. We determined the other bank had failed to help the customer with a loan when he needed money to expand his business. The other bank turned him down without showing him any ways to improve his credit quality. Before leaving, we had copies of three month's worth of bank statements in our hands as well as a follow up appointment. Our first three goals were accomplished and we were in better shape to go for the fourth.

Not only were we successful with three out of four goals on the first call, Mary experienced a tremendous sense of accomplishment from the call. Had our only goal been to get the customer in the branch to open an account that afternoon, we both would've been disappointed.

Why didn't we go for the sale on that first call? As I stated earlier, rarely does someone change banks on an impulse. It's a thoughtful decision to make. Had I allowed my new sales rep to make moving the relationship as her only goal, she would have left the prospect's office with a sense of failure. On the other hand, because we had established realistic goals, she left the prospect's office knowing she had achieved 75 percent of them.

Did we set the goals too low and not challenge ourselves since we reached most all the goals? No, not at all. The goals were attainable, but also challenging, requiring Mary to stretch herself to ask the prospect for things she would not have normally asked. The prospect raised numerous objections, which we had to overcome.

Many times a customer is very reluctant to give you copies of his confidential bank statements. People will open their doors once for a salesperson, but he better have some great ideas that will truly help the customer if a follow up call is intended. We were able to leave with copies of his bank statements and an appointment for our follow up call.

One key component in measuring the success of your goals is to make a list of them. Yes, you have heard it so many times from so many sources on so many topics to make a list of your goals.

You're sick and tired of hearing that message from your boss and everyone else. Right? But since you've heard it so often, there must be reasons why it's so important.

Writing your goals is important for several reasons. First, you know where you're headed. Every opponent is different. Every journey is different. Every Sunday afternoon on the gridiron is different. Sometimes the course is easily laid out for you while at other times it's difficult to see the course. When you list your goals, you clearly define your course and know where and how to proceed.

You list your goals because it helps you focus on the prize at the end of the game. In relating details of the earlier training call, I didn't tell you I had the list of four goals in front of me during the call. Periodically, I would glance at them. It reminded me of why Mary and I were on this call.

Customers and prospects will throw numerous curve balls at you during a call. If during the game curve balls are thrown, they can easily distract you from your goals. Having your goals on paper in front of you lets you clearly see when you cross the finish line and whether you're in first or last place.

By writing your goals, you're also able to see your successes on paper beside the goals. Let's face it. In sales we all hear *"no"* more often than we hear *"yes."* When you write down your goals and then write down your successes, you get to see and hear *"yes"* more often. What's on your scoreboard?

When your goals are realistic, attainable, challenging, and written, you have a greater chance for success. You have the opportunity to visualize success and the opportunity to celebrate the successes. Reaching goals like these won't show up on the monthly sales reports generated by your company.

These goals won't be talked about in the quarterly sales meetings either. However, the results will immediately show up in your attitude about yourself and eventually make it to those weekly, monthly, quarterly or annual reports in the form of increased sales.

So write your goals for each and every call because each and every call will be different. You need to have your game face on before stepping into a prospect's office, or before someone walks into your store, or even before you pick up the telephone to call a prospect. Making a list of goals will help you do this.

Second Quarter:
Building Your Foundation

The second quarter begins when you step into the prospect's office, when the customer walks into your place of business, or when you pick up the telephone. I refer to second quarter as the *"Building Your Foundation"* period. You may also want to refer to this period as *"making the connection."*

The connection you make should have three parts, or, stated differently, you must break the second quarter into three sub-periods. Those sub-periods are: 1) The Person; 2) The Company or Business; and finally, 3) Your Product and how to position it into the company. You should build on each of these sub-periods in the same way you build on the major ones.

Each should be helping you move into the next quarter with points already on the scoreboard while building a foundation from which you can sell your products or services.

During the first sub-period of the second quarter, you're sizing up the buyer's personality to determine what approach will be successful. One of your goals during this time should be to find common ground that will unite buyer and seller on a personal level.

Therefore, asking probing questions about the person is very important to finding common ground. Also, if you reflect on the earlier section about personalities, you'll recall that different personalities will give you different amounts of time, especially when it comes to talking about themselves.

If the time clock for this sub-period gives you a maximum of 10 minutes to discover all you can about the person seated across from you, the time granted to you by each personality may look something like the following chart.

The Quarterback and Running Back personalities like to talk about themselves the most. The Linemen will talk, but you almost have to drag it out of them. Finally, you see the Wide Receiver. Wide Receivers are the most reluctant personality to talk about themselves at the beginning of the sales call. The Wide Receiver will take longer to warm up to you and your chances of building a personal connection are greater at the end of the call. Regardless of the personality type you're dealing with, it's imperative that you make a strong personal connection between buyer and seller.

This period is meant to be relaxing and give you the opportunity to have fun getting to know your prospect. This should be a casual conversation between two or more people who are getting to know each another. The transition between the sub-periods should be as seamless to the buyer as a fast break on a basketball court is to a smooth exchange of the ball between the players as they run down the court. The ball passed between players represents an exchange of questions and answers between you and the buyer.

When you begin to ask questions of the buyer about himself, you'll want to use probing questions that require more than a *"yes"* or *"no"* answer. You should be asking questions about the person to help build or customize your presentation, and that will help you build and store information for later use.

Are those factors money, time, convenience, or what? Can you extract information when prospects talk about spouse and family that will position you to make the sale? It's like a great defensive back reading the eyes of a quarterback to know the exact spot where the ball is about to be thrown. If you can read the signs and determine the factors that influence the buyer's decision-making process, then you're much closer to closing the sale.

Buyers communicate in more ways than verbally. As you enter a prospect's office, you'll notice many different objects. Some of those objects reveal things about the buyer and can be used during the questioning time and will help build a relationship of trust as well as yield information to help sell your product. Can you uncover clues that will help you in closing the sale?

If you notice a picture of the family, then you know relationships are important to the buyer and you should strive to build a strong relationship with the buyer. If you see trophy after trophy lining the buyer's bookcases, then you'll need to feed the ego sitting across the table from you. It doesn't matter if the office is adorned with collegiate pride or is barren.

Clues about the buyer are all around. How will you use those clues and the information gathered from them? Let's face it. Selling is nothing more than finding out what motivates people to make buying decisions. When you ask personal questions, you're uncovering that person's buying motivation.

Let me help you by walking you through this sub-period as if I were making a call on a prospect. The script might look something like this:

> *"Good morning, Mr. Williams. Thank you for seeing me today."*

> **"Good morning, Allen. Thanks for stopping by."**

"How's your day going so far?"

"Fine. We're in the middle of wrapping up payroll this week and are trying to get the checks into the employees' hands on time."

Stop! There is my first clue! People are important to this buyer. He wants to make sure his employees are not inconvenienced by delayed payroll checks. He also believes in doing a job right. But how does one obtain so much information from that little response? Here he mentioned both his employees and being on time. Those words are my clues. Let's continue.

"Great. I won't waste your time this morning Mr. Williams. **(Noticing the picture on the desk.)** *Is this a picture of your grandchildren?"*

"Yes. Those are two of my four. Those two there are a lot of fun. I don't have a picture of the twins that were born last week."

Those pictures and his response confirm that Mr. Williams cares about people and those people may motivate him to buy. Therefore, continue this conversation pattern and uncover all you can about Mr. Williams and what influences his buying.

> *"They are absolutely adorable. How often do you get to spend time with them?"*

> **"Ah, I get to spend a great deal of time with them. My son works here. Their mother brings them by to visit two or three times a week after school. My wife and I keep them some on the weekends as well."**

> *"What about the twins, do they live nearby?"*

> **"Yes, my daughter and her husband live on the other side of town."**

While you may think this is chit-chat, it truly has yielded valuable information you can use to help sell your product, especially if your product includes any type of employee benefit such as life insurance, health insurance, retirement services, etc. Mr. Williams has expressed to you once again how important family and people are to him.

A simple and unnoticeable conversation that transitions from the person to the company or business should be smooth and easy. If done properly, the prospective buyer shouldn't notice you've turn the wheel to the left or right to make the curve.

> ### *"Mr. Williams, how long have you worked here at ABC Company?"*

An innocent question such as the one I just posed is simple and makes it easy to begin steering the conversation from person to company where you can begin to collect more information to prepare you for your presentation.

> **"I started here thirty-two years ago taking orders from our customers. I then moved up in the company to take on more responsibility. Now I have grown into the CFO position, I guess because nobody else wanted it."**

BINGO! Here's some more great information about the buyer. He is loyal to the company and trusted by the owner because he's been given more responsibility over the years. He's a real player in the organization.

"That's great, Mr. Williams, thirty-two years here at the company. So what have you liked most about working here at ABC?"

"I've enjoyed the opportunity it has given me to grow. Ed, the owner, has given me the flexibility to do what I need to do. If I see we need to make a change in the accounting process, he tends to support me on those changes."

HOLD ON! Mr. Williams just gave a <u>BIG</u> clue. The owner, Ed, lets Mr. Williams make his own decisions. You'll want to use this later on when Mr. Williams is hesitant to sign the agreement. You'll have to remind him of what he said: *"Ed, the owner, has given **me** flexibility to do what I need to do."* A buyer has sales Miranda rights: Anything he says can and <u>will</u> be used to sell him in the sales court room.

But let's continue to accumulate our evidence before we begin to make our presentation to Mr. Williams. Throughout this period, you want to extract as much information as you can so when you do launch your sales campaign, you'll make an impression because the buyer will feel as if you've created a custom proposal for him.

166

Remember the questions you use don't have to be complicated and shouldn't be during this time. Keep it simple and keep the conversation moving in the direction you want it to go.

> *"Mr. Williams, would you share with me more about your company?"*

> **"Well, we've been in business for over fifty years. We started with this one facility and now we are in four states and do business with more than 300 customers. We manufacture widgets and sell them through local distributors."**

Once again Mr. Williams has revealed several key pieces of information I can use to sell various financial services. Because the company has multiple locations, I have a strong opportunity to sell him direct deposit of employee pay, lockbox deposit services, information reporting, merchant direct capture, cash concentration, 401k, investments, etc. All this information was obtained in a couple of questions about the company, long before my presentation started.

By the way, did you notice how subtle I had moved from the first sub-period to the second sub-period, the company? If you can master this technique, then most of the time, the buyer won't even realize the conversation has shifted from the person to the company.

When you transition from one phase to the next, you want the transition to be invisible to the prospective buyer. You want things to appear as a simple conversation between two people. It should be like a quarterback running a play-action pass in football. You have the defense thinking run and all of a sudden it turns out to be a pass play.

You will also notice I have tried to use short probing questions to encourage the client to talk. It's important that the customer do most of the talking and for the salesperson to listen intently. Maybe you've heard of the "80/20 Rule," which applies to many things in life. On a sales call, the "80/20 rule" means that you, the salesperson, listen 80 percent of the time and talk only 20 percent of the time.

I've witnessed on numerous occasions and must admit that at times I've been guilty of the following sales sin myself. That sin is to ask multiple questions in rapid succession, never allowing the buyer to respond to any of them.

Does something like this sound familiar?

"Mr. Williams, how are you today?
Are you having a good day? I mean
is everything going okay?"

The buyer was asked the same question three times. I've seen others ask totally different questions and then answer the questions for the buyer, never giving the buyer the chance to speak at all.

> **"Mr. Williams, how are you today? You look like you're doing great. Is our company doing a good job for you? We must be. I haven't heard any complaints. Is there anything we need to be doing for you? Of course, I guess you would call us if you need something, right? Did you hear about Mr. Smith?"**

Obviously I've exaggerated this to prove a point but I've actually been on calls that were very similar to the one-sided conversation shown above. The seller used random, unfocused questions that yielded little or no information to help sell your product.

As I transition into the final sub-period to learn how to position my products or services into the company's plans, I will again try to use questions to keep the conversation flowing with useful information. These questions can start as broad, open-ended, probing questions. You must customize these questions to fit your company's products and your buyer's needs. In each industry I've worked I've used one simple question that can be used for almost any product or service and acquires a tremendous amount of information from the customer.

> *"Mr. Williams, if you could change any one thing about your current _____, what would you change?*

When I sell banking services, I use a similar question yet just as simple. Even though I know I'll receive the same answer 80 percent of the time, I still ask it because it places me in the right position to ask the next question.

> *"Mr. Williams, what services are you using through your current bank?"*

> **"We have a loan to help with the seasonality of our business, and, of course, we have a checking account."**

While this response is a static answer, it provides me with some information and helps open the door to ask the next question. It's much like a billiard player setting up the next shot.

"Are you using any special services offered by your bank?"

Notice how I continue to keep the questions uncomplicated but manage to keep the dialogue moving in the direction I want to go. I guess this is somewhat like Michael Jordan using a head fake to stall the defensive player and allow himself to maneuver to the basket.

> **"Well we use direct deposit for our employees. We call the bank each day to find out what has cleared our checking accounts and we then transfer money between our checking accounts and our revolving line of credit. It's pretty standard banking. We are not too sophisticated around here."**

Gold mine! Mr. Williams just told me he is using direct deposit but he also needs information reporting, a line of credit sweep service, and zero balance accounts. We haven't even mentioned any of those services, or the lockbox, merchant capture, and cash concentration services. I now have a referral for one of my lenders, and I have a chance to cross-sell this customer on numerous deposit and financial services; and I haven't even started my sales presentation, or have I?

The exchange of ideas I presented in the second quarter of the sales game is typical and applicable to any product or service sold. You must adjust the questions to fit your products or services, but the concept and process should remain the same:

1) get to know **the person**;
2) get to know the **company or business**; and finally,
3) get to know **how your product fits** into the company.

Your products and/or services will most likely be different than what I've shown you through the earlier dialogue. Perhaps you sell retirement investments such as 401Ks or Simple IRAs.

You may discover the buyer has a soft spot for his employees; and if so, you'll then tailor your presentation to capitalize on that emotion. On the other hand, he may not care about his employees, but only about how he can make more money. In that case, you'll want to show the buyer how your products will satisfy the need for increased returns and reduced expenses.

The purpose for this quarter, as stated earlier, is to make a connection between you and the buyer. There is also a second reason, and that's for the buyer's comfort level in you to grow while talking with you so that he is comfortable sharing his thoughts or feelings, which are factors that motivate the buyer to make a decision. Regardless of the buyer's reasons to buy, as you gather information that can help you sell your products or services you should store the information so it can be used in the fourth quarter and overtime period to help you close the sale.

Depending on the buyer's personality, the sub-periods will vary in both time and information gathered. For some buyers such as Wide Receivers and Linemen, you may have to dig a little deeper to gather the information necessary to sell your products or services. The personality I showed you in the example was a Quarterback with Running Back tendencies, a combination from which you can extract information that will help you transition to the next quarter.

As you begin to wrap up your general questions, you should focus on more specific questions about your products and how your products fit into the buyer's plans.   I refer to this period as uncovering the needs.

Third Quarter:
Uncovering the Needs

If someone were to ask me to define selling, I would define it with a two-part answer: The ability to uncover an existing need or create a need followed by the ability to present the right solution that convinces a buyer to decide to fulfill the need. First, uncovering an existing need of which the buyer was unaware, or, the creation of a new need to which the buyer has never been exposed.   The latter occurs at times when the buyer has no intention of making a purchase, but your power to push the buyer's impulse button is the ability to create a need. The second part of the definition is to present the solution and convince the buyer to act. No matter if you're exposing an existing need or creating a new one, the process for selling your product or service is the same.

You've asked questions about the person, the company, and their business as it relates overall to your relationship to buyer as well as your products or services. Now you must focus on the real needs of the buyer by asking appropriate questions. This keeps the buyer talking, thus providing information to move the buyer to a positive decision.

Regardless of the product or service I represent, I always start this quarter by asking the question I mentioned moments ago to every prospect I meet. If the services are banking, the question is simple: "Mrs. Clark, if you could change one thing about your banking, what would that be?"

Of course, this question most always triggers a first response of, "Lower my loan rates," or, "Raise my CD rates."

But I quickly move on from that response and get back to the original question: "If you could change one thing about your banking, what would that be?"

It's an open-ended question that yields information for honing in on the products I'm seeking to sell the buyer.

I've mentioned the movie *Hoosiers* where actor Gene Hackman plays the role of Coach Norman Dale, a high school basketball coach, who doesn't allow the players to shoot the ball until after they pass the ball at least four times.

If you understand the game of basketball, you know the reason for four passes is to break down the defense of the other team and create an open shot. Selling works the same way; you must break the buyer's defenses down in order to make the sale. A salesperson should never shoot the ball until he has made at least four passes or cleared the defense.

What I mean by this is you should ask four questions before you attempt to present your solution. Why? Because in the same way a basketball team attempts to break down the defenses of the opposing team, you're trying to break down the defenses of the buyer, or put different, you're trying to expose the need.

You ask questions that relate to the company's use, or potential use, of your product or service. Those questions help reveal the buyer's "hot buttons," or reasons for making the decision. As you ask those questions, gauge the buyer's responses and determine the features and benefits most appealing to the buyer. Then use the same responses when you present the solution and remind the buyer of his hot buttons.

How do you know when you have enough information and can stop asking questions and present your solution? You continue to ask questions until you know you have all the needs uncovered and you know what the buyer's hot buttons are. As long as you're receiving positive answers from the customer, you have permission to continue probing.

Look at it this way. During an offensive series in a football game, the team playing offense is given four downs to move the ball ten yards and earn another first down, score a touchdown, kick a field goal, or give up and punt the ball. Now we all know the first three options are most desirable. If you were a personal computer sales rep and were given four downs, or questions, on a sales call, the series of questions may be as follows:

1st & 10: *"Mr. Adams, how many computers does your company use at this office?"*

Response: "We have somewhere around thirty in this office."

Nice play. You just picked up three yards.

2nd & 7: *"Mr. Adams, are you satisfied with your current hardware provider?"*

Response: "Yeah, I guess so. We have been with them for fifteen years now."

Ouch! You're sacked behind the line of scrimmage. You just lost two yards. It's now third and long and you're in a passing situation. What big play, or question, will you use next to keep the ball advancing forward?

> **3rd & 9:** *"Mr. Adams, how well connected are your computers to one another and how easy is it to share information from one user to the next?"*

> **Response: "Well, that's a problem. We have no connectivity between the computers and that slows us down a great deal."**

Great move! You just picked up eight yards on that play.

> **4th & 1:** *"Mr. Adams, can I show you how our company can help you overcome that connectively problem and provide you with competitive prices?"*

> **Response: "Absolutely!"**

First down and congratulations! You have permission from the buyer to continue asking questions that will help you present a solution and sell your product or service.

Fourth Quarter:
Presenting the Right Solution

When presenting your solution, you first have to look back at the buyer's Miranda Rights. Your "Court of Sales" has been called to order and what the buyer stated earlier should now be used as you present your solution. What do I mean by using what the buyer said as you present your solution? Throughout the first three quarters, the buyer revealed deal-closing information, which you stored in your mind; and it's now time for you to use the buyer's own words against him, so-to-speak, to help make your case for the right solution. Here is how it works.

You're selling copier machines, and during the first three quarters you uncover the buyer isn't happy with the service the current vendor provides. You also discover the buyer wants to be able to load more paper into the machine for bigger jobs and he wants to use 8.5" x 11" paper at the same time he uses 8.5" x 14" paper. The buyer has told you his three "hot buttons," and now it's time to remind the buyer of them.

"Kevin, you stated earlier that your current vendor has at times let you down on service. You also said the

179

features that most interest you in a new copier are a large paper capacity and the ability to copy both letter and legal size pages simultaneously. Is that right?"

"Yes. Those are the most important items for us."

The buyer already said these things, but it's important for you to restate them to the buyer for the following reasons:

> 1. Confirm you understand what the buyer seeks;
>
> 2. Remind the customer what's important to him -- his hot buttons;
>
> 3. Ensure the buyer is still listening and interacting with you.

You have rephrased the buyer's words and now you're absolutely sure about the buyer's needs or wants. You can begin presenting your solution.

Your copiers have countless features and benefits, and now is the time to tell the buyer about every last one of them. Right? Yes, if you want to blow the deal. No, if you want to make the sale.

You should focus on the features that most interest the buyer. But if the buyer asks, "What else can your copier do?" Then you can relate the other features and their benefits. Let's look at how our salesman might present features which interest the buyer.

> *"Kevin, you said service is extremely important to you, and it should be. My company has more than 2,000 copiers in service here in town, and almost 7,000 statewide. We have technicians available 24 hours, 7 days a week to help you when you need us. One of my customers, Mr. Smith at XYZ Company, has been using our copiers for more than ten years, and he can vouch for the reliability of our equipment and the expediency with which we fix them in the event something goes wrong. In fact, here is my client list, any of whom will tell you how satisfied they are with our company's products and services. Do you recognize anyone on the list?"*

"This is an impressive list. Yes, I know Bob at _____."

In these few sentences, you have reminded the customer of what's important to him. You have provided a verifiable testimonial from a *real* customer. And, most important, you concluded with a question to keep the buyer engaged in the conversation. Any time you present a feature, be sure the customer agrees with you on that feature by asking a confirmation question.

The second feature important to the customer is a large capacity paper holder. As the copier salesperson, you may have numerous models to choose from.

Instead of enumerating every model copier in your inventory, narrow the choices to what meet your customer's stated needs.

> *"Mr. Adams, you also said you wanted a copier with a dual-size paper capacity large enough to complete any size copying job without stopping. Our BC2500 model is capable of holding 2,000 sheets of 8.5" x 11" paper and 500 sheet of 8.5" x 14" paper. Will this be enough for most of your large copying jobs?"*

Notice the solutions are concise. Maybe your products are more complicated than a copier and require more detail. Even so, don't complicate the sales process with superfluous information.

Buyers want precise, pertinent solutions that meet their needs and solutions they understand. The more complicated the solution, the less likely you are to make a sale and you will drag out the sales cycle by doing so.

You have covered two of the buyer's hot buttons. The third one helps determine if it's time to close the deal.

> *"Kevin, one of the best features about the BC2500 is exactly what you said you needed. It has the ability to print both letter and legal size documents simultaneously. The built-in sensors determine the paper size you need and automatically copy your documents to your specifications. This feature can save you a great deal of money if you only have a couple of pages that are 8.5" by 14". How does that sound, Kevin?"*

If Kevin's response to your confirmation question, "How does that sound, Kevin," is positive, then you should confidently remind Kevin your product meets all three of his needs, and then seek agreement to move forward with the sale.

> *"Kevin, I've shown you my company will provide you top quality service 24/7. The BC2500's large capacity bin will accommodate most of your copying needs with regard to quantity and different sizes. Wouldn't you agree that my company and this copier can handle your needs?"*

Whether Kevin responds positively showing he is ready for the close, or negatively with an objection, you've just moved into the overtime period, the time to close the deal.

Overtime – Closing the Sale

If you have done the right things in the first four quarters, then overtime should be easy because you've collected all the information you need to proceed with a successful close.

Overcoming Objections

Continuing on from the copier sales from the fourth quarter, let's assume Kevin responded negatively. The first and most important fact you should know about an objection is an objection isn't the customer saying; *"No, I will not buy this product from you."*

An objection is an opportunity either to clarify what the customer's needs are or a misunderstanding about your product.

I remember training a young sales rep, Connie, while on a sales call to the general manager of two car dealerships. Connie breezed through the first four quarters of the call as if she were Atlanta Falcon's quarterback Matt Ryan connecting with Roddy White, and things were looking good. She was demonstrating a feature that addressed one of the customer's hot button needs when the customer changed directions and asked, "How much is it?"

As Connie was answering the question, the buyer screamed, "You've gotta be kiddin' me! Thirty-five bucks a month for this?"

Note the buyer didn't scream, "I will not pay this price!"

What the buyer was intimating was this: "Justify to me why I should pay your price."

So Connie justified the price to the customer.

As trained, Connie used the buyer's own hot button words from the first four quarters to prove the value of the service.

TOUCHDOWN!

We left with agreements for both dealerships and four accounts.

When handling objections many salespeople use the "feel, felt, found" formula. While this formula works, I'm convinced that the feel, felt, found, **FINALIZE** formula works even better.

What do I mean by feel, felt, found, finalize?

FEEL – Express to the customer you understand and empathize with his or her feeling, for example:

"Kevin, I understand how you might feel this copier is too expensive."

FELT – Show the buyer he isn't the first to ever feel this same way: "I've had other customers express the same concern to me."

FOUND – Use verifiable testimonials of others who overcame the concern, bought your product or service, and who were pleased: "After they saw how well our copiers performed for them, they quickly realized the machines pay for themselves."

It's the same process you've been trained to do from the beginning of your sales career but the most important component is to confirm the buyer agrees with you.

Therefore, you must finalize the process.

FINALIZE – Make sure you have who overcome the objection by asking a finalizing question: "Kevin, do you see how our copier can help you?"

Let's put it all together so you can see how the entire response to the objection flows.

> *"Kevin, I understand how you might feel this copier is too expensive. I've had other customers express the same concern to me. But upon observing how well our copiers performed and our commitment to service, they quickly realized the machines pay for themselves. Kevin, do you see how our copier can help you?"*

By adding one more step, you can overcome the objection and begin to finalize the sale. And how many of us in sales haven't had to overcome a pricing objection. Not having to face the pricing objection is just as ridiculous as a wide receiver not having to face a defensive backfield. I hope you can see from the response I've used how you can use this technique for any objection to any product or service.

Asking for the business

If at the end of the fourth quarter the buyer is responding positively, finalize the deal by asking, *"Kevin, can we move forward with this decision?"*

If Kevin responds negatively at this point, you'll need to uncover and overcome the objections as discussed in the previous section. On the other hand, if Kevin responds positively, then you should thank Kevin for his positive response and ask him to sign the paperwork. NEVER hesitate at this point.

If you do, the buyer may think he's making the wrong decision. Keep the process moving ahead at a good pace. However, don't rush the customer. Take it at a steady pace in which the buyer is comfortable, but do make sure you are moving forward.

I remember my first month in a previous job. The gentleman training me accompanied me on a sales call. I employed the techniques I've shared with you. I set my goals. I built my foundation with the customer. I uncovered his need. I presented the right solution using the buyer's words and I walked out with the agreement.

When the gentleman and I returned to the car he said, *"I've never seen that happen before in my life."* I thought to myself, *"Oh no! What did I do wrong?"* I asked: *"What had you not seen before?"* Steve said that he'd never seen a prospect make a purchase on the first sales call. My expectation and plan was to make the sale and that's what I did.

During the close, don't allow yourself or the buyer to become distracted by something else. Keep the buyer engaged and reassure their positive decisions by once again using their words.

> *"Kevin, you're making a great decision. You'll be extremely happy with the service we provide. You're going to be amazed at the ease of using the BC2500."*

Once the deal is made, don't step out of bounds by overselling your product or service. I've seen time and time again where a salesperson would try to keep selling the customer long after the sale was made. Overselling most commonly happens by continuing to tell the customer relating features not discussed during the presentation. You know the ones, those features you know and like but aren't important to the buyer.

It doesn't matter if you like the features or think they are important. If the buyer doesn't need those features, then don't waste the buyer's time and yours by stepping out of bounds and overselling.

If you're playing offense in a basketball game, you'll be penalized for standing in the paint for three or more seconds. And if you hit a baseball outside the baselines, it's both a foul and a strike. Unfortunately the boundaries of a sales call are not as clearly defined as in basketball or baseball.

In fact, the boundaries change with each new call and each new player or prospect. It's often difficult to interpret where the boundaries lie. You cannot always prepare fully for the call, because until you set foot in the arena, you may know very little about the game or the person to whom you're selling.

As previously indicated, I enjoy watching Formula One racing. As a grand prix continues, tire degradation causes large amounts of rubber, called marbles or clag, to pile up along the outer edges of the track just off the race line.

Even though these rubber marbles are still on the racecourse itself, drivers know that moving too far off line can cause disastrous results.

These pieces of rubber, though they were originally part of the tires on the cars, create a tremendous hazard when a driver runs over them. The marbles quickly adhere to the car's hot tires, thus changing the tires' balance and the car's handling. Steering becomes more difficult. If a driver is not careful, the marbles can cause wrecks or even death.

It's sometimes difficult to see the marbles, but drivers know they're there. It's also difficult to see the rubber marbles in a prospect's office. In either case the results can be the same: you lose the race and you lose the sale. So then, how do you see the excess rubber on the course? How do you know here the boundaries lie?

To determine the boundaries of your sales call, you must constantly assess the environment of the sale call. Ask yourself, "How is my audience responding to me?" Do you have the buyer's attention? Have you talked about features that aren't important to the buyer, causing the buyer to disengage in the conversation? If any of your answers are negative, then you're heading for the marbles.

Like a Formula One driver, you must react quickly but gently to regain control of the car or in your case, the sale.

If after picking up rubber marbles and getting the car out of shape, a Grand Prix driver presses the gas pedal too hard the marbles will likely send the rear end of the car spinning around. On the other hand, hitting the brakes too hard may cause the wheels to lock up and could send the driver completely off course.

If as a salesperson, you hit the gas and find you are talking about features that are not important to the buyer, then slow down and refocus back on the features that are important.

The opposite from pressing the gas pedal is to hit the brakes. During a sales presentation you recognize you are talking about features that do not interest the buyer, do not stop abruptly. Gently work your way back on course as opposed to slamming the brakes. Refocus the buyer by reminding him of the features that had them interested in your product.

The boundaries for a sales call are different each time. A salesperson must constantly reevaluate each buyer to determine the features that are important to the buyer.

Remember to ask engaging questions to keep your audience in tact and on the same page with you. Whether you're making a presentation to one or 1,000, engaging the audience while inbounds will help you close the sale. If you know you're in bounds and the buyer is connected with you, then close the sale.

Once you close the sale, make sure you help set and meet your buyer's expectations. Nothing damages future sales opportunities more than failing to meet expectations.

When I set expectations with a buyer, I always over estimate the time it will take to deliver. I always under estimate the savings I can offer a customer. Yes, I've lost a couple of deals this way. But guess what? By setting realistic expectations, prospects have always come back around in my favor.

Here's just one example: a few years ago, I met with a prospect who believed my company was too small to handle the needs of his company, so he chose a larger vendor. Two years later, I won his business because the previous vendor of choice over-promised and under-delivered.

I did the opposite.

I gave honest estimates that assured me I could deliver product and service beyond the customer's expectations. This company became on of my largest clients and followed me to a competitor company.

The final piece of your close is to follow up on a customer or new buyer. During the implementation phase you should assure the buyer that things are progressing as planned.

Once again, reassure the buyer he has made the right decision and remind him of the benefits.

After the service or product has been delivered, you should follow up with the buyer. This is all a part of closing this sale as well as garnering future sales he'll give you directly or in the form of referrals. Follow up with your buyers even after the commission has been paid.

Chapter 6

Conclusion

Throughout this book, I've shared with you methods and ideas that have worked for me as a sales rep for three completely different products over the past 25 years. Most of the techniques I've discussed are not new. You may have heard them time and time again. My goal has not been to reveal some new secrets that will make you instantly successful in sales.

My goal has been two-fold: First, I wanted to remind you of those tried-and-true techniques. Over the years, I've had great success in utilizing the thoughts and ideas I've shared with you. I hope you discover ways to use these techniques in your career each and every day. Second, placing age-old techniques in a sports context allows many readers to relate to and remember them, and also to use them. By paralleling those proven methods with sports analogies, I hope you have been encouraged and entertained. But most important, I hope you have found new ways to be successful in your career as a salesperson.

But before we finish, let's recap the techniques and the steps discussed in the book.

☑ Who are You and Who is Your Buyer?

You have learned there are four basic personalities. You have learned there are also infinite combinations of personality traits. How will you deal with each one? Each of us has our own personality and our own unique ways to interpret what goes on around us. If you want to have a successful career in sales, you should make understanding people your top priority.

It's important to know the person or people sitting across the table from you and to understand what motivates each buyer. It's equally important you know and understand yourself. You should be objective and introspective when determining changes to increase your productivity.

☑ Know the Product

Whether you're just beginning your career in sales or have been selling for 30 years, you should constantly reeducate yourself on your products and services. We live in an ever-changing world, and to think our products and services don't change is begging for your career to be over. You must review the features and benefits of your products and services routinely.

Your products change and so do those of your competition. You must know your competition completely if you want to succeed. One can never learn all there is to know about one's competitors. If you don't know the competition's latest products and services, it is time you learn them. Make sure you know as much about your competition as you know about yourself.

You should know the dominant and lesser features of your products and those of your competition. Once you know the various features then learn how to convert those features into benefits for your customers. The more you know about your products and how they can help your customers, the more likely you'll have a long successful career in sales.

☑ Place Yourself Where the Leads Are

Leads are all around you. Your job is to position yourself and extend your arms to receive those leads. There are two primary sources of leads for us, internal and external. Internal leads are those shared across company lines or departments.

Internal leads are typically the easiest to receive, but often are lost because of territorial disputes with other divisions or players. Our own customer base is a tremendous source of leads many of us often overlook.

External leads take on many different shapes. They too are all around you. Your existing customers have vendors, customers and competitors. Each of these can be a source of external leads. Trade associations, publications, conventions, etc., are excellent resources for uncovering new leads. The possibilities seem almost endless no matter what products you sell.

☑ Set Your Goals

Planning the call has many facets. You first have to know what you intend to say and what you intend to accomplish. You have to anticipate the objections that will come up during the presentation and plan how you'll handle those objections. Writing a list of your goals for the call is paramount to the success of the call. Once you have those things in order, you must practice, practice, practice.

☑ Implement the Plan

When you arrive at the prospect's office you must be prepared to implement your plan and make adjustments to your offense as the call moves forward. You must make the connection with the buyer while engaging the buyer in productive conversation.

Constantly reevaluate this level of connection to ensure buyer agreement.

Build your foundation by asking probing questions that yield information about the buyer and what motivates him to buy.

☑ Ask for the Business

You should remind the buyer of the factors that are most important to him as they relate to your product or service. The buyer knows his Miranda Rights. So now use his words to help close the sale. When using the "Feel, Felt, Found" approach to overcoming objections you need to remember to include the "Finalize" step as well. Ask a finalizing, or confirming question to ensure you overcame the objection.

Once you overcome all objections, close the deal without stepping out of bounds by overselling. If a feature provides no benefit to the customer, then don't mention it unless the buyer asks.

You should set realistic expectations on the part of the buyer. Over-promising and under-delivering is devastating and will cost you more future sales than you can imagine. Make sure you and the buyer understand the expectations.

☑ Follow through the Sale

Reassure the buyer he has made an excellent decision. You should do this at the time the sale is made as well as throughout the implementation phase. Continue to follow up with the customer until the he is completely satisfied with your products and services.

Your follow up with a buyer after the sale is a sure way to generate additional sales from the buyer and to pick up new leads for future sales.

Most of all have fun when making sales calls. If you're not having fun and if you don't enjoy your work, then what's the point of having a career in sales? Make sure you have fun with your job each and every day.

It's my sincere hope that some technique or idea you read in this book will help propel you to the next level in your sales career. I wish you the very best in selling to your existing clients as well as discovering prospects everywhere you turn.

What will you do from here?

How many times have you been to a seminar, a conference, or a sales meeting where you were fired up at that moment but then let the fire go out on the way home? How many books have you read that caused you to swell with excitement and new motivation to conquer the world?

I don't know if my book has inspired you at all. If it didn't, I apologize, and I can't believe you're still reading. If, on the other hand, this book is useful to you, then, what will you do next?

Several years ago, I was listening to Jack Taylor, a Baptist minister. Taylor was talking about an event in the Book of Kings found in the Bible as well as the Talmud that reads as follows:

> *"Now there were four leprous men at the entrance of the gate; and they said to one another, "Why do we sit here until we die? If we say 'We will enter the city,' then the famine is in the city and we shall die there; and if we sit here, we die also. Now therefore come, and let us go over to the camp of the Arameans. If they*

spare us, we shall live; and if they
kill us, we shall but die."[1]

These four men had a choice to make that meant life or death for them. You, too, have a choice to make about the life and death of your career as a salesperson. Taylor pointed out the four decisions made by the lepers and applied those four decisions to the Christian faith. I believe those four decisions can also be applied to us as fathers, mothers, brothers, sisters, husbands, wives, friends, etc., and even sales representatives.

The four decisions made by the men were this:

1. We cannot stay here.

2. We cannot go back.

3. We must go forward.

4. We must tell someone.

Just as the lepers, if we do nothing with what we've read, our lives as sales reps won't improve. I've only written the words. It's your job to put them into action. So, you cannot stay here.

If you have now read this book and decide not to use any ideas found herein, then you're going

---

[1] 2 Kings 7.3-4 (NASB).

backward. If you choose to go backward and not use any information gained from what you have read, then the time spent in reading this book has been dead time. So don't go back to the place in your career you were.

The four leprous men decided to march directly into the camp of the opposing army. They went forward. You must go forward. You have the opportunity to conquer the opposition on the other side of the table from you with your newfound sales techniques. You must go forward and be successful with what you have learned.

Yes, you'll face times of failure, but you must continue toward making more sales.

The Bible says the four lepers approached the camp of the enemy and found it deserted. They also found food, drink, clothing, silver, and gold -- more than they had ever imagined.

The risk of going forward was great. But the reward for going forward was much greater. You must go forward in your career as a sales rep.

Later, the four leprous men decided to go and tell the king's household about the riches God had supplied them. You too must share your successes with someone. Your family should be the first ones with whom you share your successes.

Then let everyone around you know about your successes. Not in an arrogant way, but in a way that encourages others to strive for success also. You must tell someone how you've succeeded.

Score Board

Successes	Failures
43	*32*

Qtr: 4   Time: 0:00

Winners & Losers

ABOUT THE AUTHOR

A native of Fayetteville, North Carolina, Allen Guy attended Emmanuel College in Franklin Springs, Georgia, before enrolling in the University of Georgia and graduating with a degree in economics. Upon graduation Guy entered the business world determined to build a successful career in sales. Now with a sales and management career spanning more than twenty-five years and three industries, he has taken the lessons learned and compiled a resource through which young men and women can launch or expand their own sales career. He lives near Jackson, Mississippi, where he is employed by a leading bank.